KILLERS ON THE ROAD TO VEGAS

Ronald E Bowers

Former Senior Prosecutor
Los Angeles County District Attorney's Office

Some names and locations have been changed to protect the privacy of individuals connected with this story. Certain events have been inferred from the facts of these cases. Some quotes and dialogue have been changed for brevity.

Ronald E. Bowers, Publisher
losangelestruecrime@aol.com

ISBN 978-1-7326655-1-4

Second release February 2017

INTRODUCTION

I wrote this book, ***Killers on the Road to Vegas***, because I felt that the Shane Huang and Benjamin Frandsen case was such a double tragedy. The impact to the victims' families was greater than catastrophic. Even the suspects were tragic losers. In my 43 years as a prosecutor. I have never seen so many young men's lives become so totally devastated. I kept asking myself, "How could all this heartbreak totally destroy such young souls who had so much to live for?" However, this case touched a raw nerve of emotion in all of us. It's hard to find words to comfort those who have to continue to persevere with their daily tasks as their minds are constantly bombarded by flashbacks of their loved ones. While working on this case, I had the occasion to meet the young victims' mothers. I was never so impressed as I was by these two remarkable mothers. Their ceaseless love for their sons caused them to attempt to move heaven and earth to see that Justice was done for them. Without their tenacity, the two 'killers on the road' would never have been caught and prosecuted. Thank God for everlasting maternal love.

Many times, Missing Persons cases don't have a happy ending. I know how difficult it is for concerned family members to find the right agency to investigate the disappearance of their loved ones. In a Missing Persons situation you don't always know exactly where they disappeared. Often it is unclear which law enforcement agency to contact just to file the initial Missing Person's report. Obviously, the police agency doesn't want to spend their investigative resources if they have no nexus to the person's disappearance. In this case, the mothers didn't know for sure where their sons went missing. When the local police departments weren't willing and able to get involved, the mothers in desperation went to the FBI for assistance. As busy as the FBI is, a sympathetic agent listened to the mothers' plight. (Seldom do the words 'sympathetic' and 'FBI agent' occur together)

This story is about several dedicated FBI agents who went the extra mile to catch the callous killers. The agents could have found valid excuses to tell the victims' mothers this wasn't the type of case the FBI handled. But remarkably, these agents recognized the desperation felt by these two mothers and agreed to an initial review of the matter. These agents used their investigative skills to track down cellphone records that led to certain witnesses who helped piece together this puzzling case. What is so amazing about this case is how everything had to come together precisely at the right time. It was like having the sun, planets, and moon all come into perfect alignment for the evidence to point to the killers.

I, the author, wouldn't be able to relate to you, the reader, this incredible story if certain things hadn't occurred. It all started on a nondescript day after lunch. I was asked by one of the DA Major Crimes Division prosecutors, Karla Kerlin, to attend a meeting about an unusual case that the FBI wanted the DA's Office to take a look at. When I walked into the meeting I was introduced to two FBI agents, David Clouse (Pseudonym) and Kelly Dempsey (Pseudonym). I surmised this was going to be another fraud case, with thousands of documents, which I would have to spend weeks organizing. My experience with FBI cases is that they are ***BORING***. I find that it is challenging for me to make them interesting for jurors to understand.

Karla started the meeting by telling everyone she has been handed off this case since the deputy DA who had it was starting a lengthy trial and couldn't try it. Karla announced she only had several weeks before trial and she wanted me to prepare the exhibits and charts for the trial. I mentioned that was short notice and requested that someone tell me something about the case. I expected to hear something about a 'Paper Case' with boxes of documents, but she said that this was a **DOUBLE MURDER**. The surprised look on my face caused Karla to explain that on rare occasions the FBI did handle homicide cases. I thought to myself that, in my lengthy career as a prosecutor, I couldn't remember any murder case investigated by the FBI.

I kept my mouth shut and went into the 'Listening Mode' as Karla said that two young Israeli men had disappeared and the FBI had investigated the case. After 45 minutes of listening to the prosecutor and the agents discuss the case, I said, "We are going to need timelines to explain the facts to the jury." At that point, I said that if the agents could provide me with a 'Murder Book,' I would go to my office and get started. Every homicide case presented to the DA's Office from LAPD and the Sheriff's Homicide contains several sets of a 'Murder Book,' which have all the reports listed by category, such as Coroner, Ballistics, DNA evidence, witnesses, etc.

Then a hush went over the room. I explained that I didn't need the 'Murder Book' for long, but only for a few days. Karla in her most diplomatic voice said, "Ron, the FBI doesn't prepare 'Murder Books.'" I said, "What, no 'Murder Book?'' Karla glanced at me, showing a little displeasure with my reaction. I quickly tried to compose myself. I was receiving vibes from Karla that I should treat the FBI agents like guests and not try to embarrass them for not preparing a 'Murder Book.'

The agents tried to explain that they had all their reports but they were listed in chronological order as to when they were written. I thought, what a stupid way of organizing investigative material. In order to find something in their box of files, one needed to remember the date the report was prepared. I thought to myself, "How the hell will I ever find a report," since there is no way I as prosecutor would know when that report was written. I took a deep breath and put a smile on my face. I politely said, "Okay give me what you have on the case and I will get started." I could see they did things differently and that Karla and I would have to adapt to their ways.

What I learned from this one case was the dedication of the FBI agents and that their teamwork effort was incredible. The FBI agents couldn't have been more helpful. When I needed any information for the creation of exhibits, they supplied it ASAP (As Soon As Possible). Often, the old-time Homicide Detectives I have dealt with throughout my career have been helpful, but they always made it seem like they were doing me a favor when supplying me information that I needed to prepare their murder cases.

Another demonstration of dedication came from Karla Kerlin, the trial prosecutor. She and I reviewed what was needed to convince a jury that the defendant, Shane Huang, did the killing. She had great instincts as to what was needed, and we created visual aids that supported her theory of the case. Karla's background as a stage performer made her a natural for knowing when and how to use visual aids to tell the story to the jury.

The courtroom drama became intense, as a high-priced defense attorney knew just where the prosecution was vulnerable. The DA's witnesses had been friends with the defendant, who had just received his MBA from UCLA. If this case were to be decided on the basis of which side had the highest IQ level, there would be no doubt that the defense would win it hands down. During the trial, both attorneys vigorously tried the case. But at the time of final argument the gloves came off and verbal bareknuckle fighting commenced, which left the courtroom highly charged and led to a surprising result.

The ***Killers on the Road to Vegas*** is a book about two parents' undying love for their children, creative FBI agents who were tenacious, and a highly talented prosecutor who wouldn't accept the word 'defeat.' Their quest for Justice united them in one of the most astonishing stories to ever come out of the annals of the Los Angeles Superior Courts.

This is another book contained in my **L. A. True Crime series**, which reviews some of the most fascinating and mesmerizing cases to pass through the Los Angeles County District Attorney's Office. Over my lengthy career as a prosecutor and later in my position as Head Deputy of the Trial Support Division, I worked on or assisted in the prosecution of some intriguing and captivating cases that have a story to be told about the good and the bad of our American Criminal Justice System that the public needs to know more about.

(The following graphic page shows photos of the defendants and the victims. As there are sets of two, it is helpful for the reader to become familiar with the various names, since they will be used throughout the book.)

Graphic 1

PARTIES IN CASE
Defendants
Shane Huang
He rented house where Marijuana was grown
Benjamin Frandsen
He was friend of Huang & wanted to help him out
Victims
Ben Wertzberger
He was caring for Huang's Marijuana business
Adar Ne'eman
He came from Israel to visit with Wertzberger

CONTENTS

CHAPTER 1—SEARCHING FOR A BLUE-ROOFED BUILDING

Benjamin Frandsen (henceforth he will be referred to by his last name) didn't want to divulge where the bodies were buried in the desert. He only conceded to the FBI agents that if someone wanted to uncover the buried bodies, the place to look would be off the main highway linking Los Angeles to Vegas. His crime partner had a familiarity with this desolate area, since he had attended a Rave concert in that area. When pressed, Frandsen furnished one more clue: the bodies could be found hidden in a campground, just off the freeway.

The agents felt so near but so far from unraveling a multiple-murder case. What could they say or do to make the suspect open up and be more revealing? It seemed like a cat-and-mouse game, but with no winners. It resulted in a 'mind contest' in which the suspect tantalized the agents by giving them only tidbits. They realized they would have to do a little dance around the facts in hopes he would expose and divulge a card they could play. Whenever they got close to prying out a salient fact, Frandsen would clam up and withdraw into his emotional shell. He could feel his world imploding around him and his future crashing into oblivion. All he wanted to do was say as little as possible in hopes this was merely a bad dream that would soon be over.

Repeatedly, he assured the agents of his desire to cooperate in deciphering the mystery of the disappearance of these two young Israeli men. When asked specifics regarding the campground, Frandsen couldn't or wouldn't give them a name, or even a highway turnoff. Did he want to be evasive? Or, or possibly, he couldn't remember the details of that early morning dawn ten months earlier. The FBI agents had struggled for hours to extract specifics from the suspect, Frandsen, who continued to be cagey in providing the secrets of a dual homicide, in exchange for more lenient treatment for himself.

The agents were desperate to dig up any information where the victims' bodies could be found. The victims' Israeli parents had been riding an emotional roller coaster for ten months in an effort to find their missing sons. Closure for the parents could be possible if only Frandsen would tell the agents where the bodies could be recovered.

Nine hours of interrogation had drained the agents of their eagerness to play a game of tit for tat. Had their efforts resulted in acquiring some valuable information, or had they been suckered into a wild story from a scared murder suspect who was being held in a lonely ranger station somewhere in Yellowstone National Park?

As the jailers led Frandsen away, he turned to the agents and said, "Look for a blue-roofed building with internet letters 'www' across the top." As he vanished from view, the two agents looked at each other. Agent Clouse said, "What do you make of that?" Agent Kelly Dempsey shook her head in disbelief and said, "What did we really learn from him?" Their reaction had to be that this was the strangest set of directions they had ever elicited from a suspect.

In reviewing their notes, the agents had been able to elicit from the suspect several significant facts. The bodies were buried near a campground, in the desert off Interstate 15 Freeway somewhere between Los Angeles and Las Vegas. That didn't narrow down the search by much. Would the added fact that the turnoff was near a building with a blue roof and an internet sign on top be of any benefit to finding a gravesite?

The agents had a regrouping moment of deciphering what material they did have. Did they have enough info to send out a search party? If so, where do they start? One of the agents trying to exhibit resourcefulness indicated that someone should contact the California Highway Patrol (CHP), since they are in charge of patrolling the freeways in California. Their officers regularly patrol the I-15 Freeway dozens of times a day and night, so maybe one of the officers would recognize the nebulous description. The FBI agents made contact with the CHP station near Barstow.

The agent called the CHP station and asked for some help in locating a turnoff from the I-15 Freeway. In a hesitant voice, the agent said, "Are you familiar with an off-ramp near a building with a blue roof, with a web site name on top." The agent sensed a slight degree of embarrassment in his making of such a general inquiry and expected the CHP officer to be dismissive. However, the CHP officer on duty didn't chuckle at the request and, in a matter-of-fact voice said, "Do you mean the 'Afton Canyon Campground' turnoff?" The CHP officer may have been working the desert beat too long to find anything peculiar. "Where exactly is it?" the FBI agent responded. "It's about halfway between Barstow and Baker," the officer replied.

With that information, the race was on to see if a needle could be found in a haystack. The area in question encompasses a portion of the Mojave Desert stretching 63 miles from Barstow to Baker. Every weekend thousands of gamblers take this route to Las Vegas. To many, this is like a pilgrimage in hopes of finding their fortune hidden somewhere in the bowels of a flashy casino. The high rollers are forced to endure this tedious section of road just to be able to arrive at a gambler's paradise. This monotonous stretch of roadway gives the traveler a chance to gaze out of their vehicle's window at nothingness for as far as the eye can see.

The FBI arranged for two helicopters to be made available to them. Agent David Kidd jumped aboard the lead copter; the other was to follow it with a photographer to take photos of whatever they may uncover. In short order they flew over the City of Barstow, noticing the railroad hub that historically made this place a city. The famous Harvey House, with its Spanish-Moroccan design, still stands next to the main railroad tracks. In 1908, Fred Harvey built this hotel-restaurant to provide a more luxurious way to travel. The waitresses wore distinctive white uniforms, and history remembers them as the 'Harvey Girls.' Today the Route 66 historical museum has turned it into a visitors stop.

As the copter trekked on, the FBI agent exhibited no interest in gazing on the history below as they continued over the junction of the Interstate 15 and 40 Freeways. At this altitude, these highways looked like spools of ribbons unraveling into a vast barren landscape. After leaving Barstow, one could faintly see ahead the letters "CALICO" painted on the hillside. Within moments, the eye is treated to a colorful hodgepodge of reds, oranges, and grays streaming down the hillside. This cascade of color is from the remaining ore oozing out of the old abandoned mines.

Today Calico is a ghost town and tourist attraction, but back in the 1880's it claimed to be the largest silver producer in California. The city boomed with a population of 1200, until the Silver Purchase Act drove silver prices down to the point where mining was unprofitable. The miners left as quickly as they had arrived, resulting in a skeleton of a city. The only reminder of the old mining town is the dilapidated wooden buildings, a saloon, general store, hotel and a train station which were all a part of the true Wild West.

Nostalgia had to be put aside as the agent zoomed his binoculars in on the various off-ramps from the freeway. Every exit had some type of structure mainly appealing to the throngs heading to Vegas. Be it service stations or restaurants, they dotted the countryside. At one off-ramp, "Peggy Sues," a 50s diner, can be seen with tour buses packed into a dirt-filled parking lot. Its roof would be described as a dull gray, but as to the other buildings, the agent couldn't clearly determine the color of the roofs. The agent indicated to the pilot that they needed to fly lower. The helicopter dipped lower, making sightings of the structures easier. Were they on a wild goose chase or about to strike it rich, so to speak, by finding the victims' bodies?' As they distanced themselves from Barstow, the off-ramps were seldom, and some were in the middle of nowhere. How does one describe emptiness? Several off-ramps came and went, but no blue-roofed building.

Vaguely, in the distance, the agent saw a building with a pale-blue roof. As they flew closer, they could see the letters on top of the roof: WWW.JEFFCHRIS.COM. They didn't know if that was what Frandsen was talking about. They couldn't be certain, but it did incorporate two of the requirements. As the helicopter orbited overhead, the agent instructed the pilot to make a wide circle around the blue-roofed building, hoping to see a campground.

(On the following graphic page is the statement made by Frandsen regarding looking for the blue roofed building. Also, there is the exhibit of the map showing the road to Vegas from Barstow to Baker.)

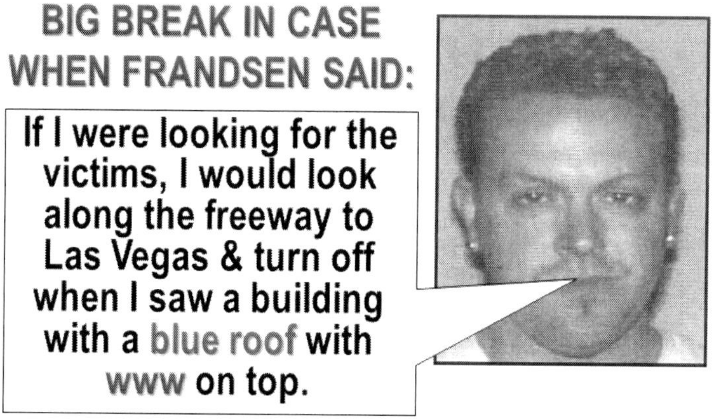

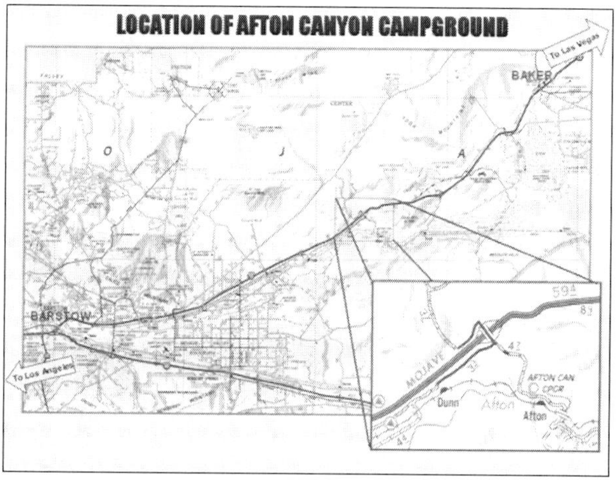

CHAPTER 2—SEARCHING FOR THE GRAVESITE

A paved road curved away from the freeway and became narrower and appeared impassable as it deteriorated into a dirt road. The word 'rugged' would best describe this road to nowhere. Even from the helicopter, boulders could be spotted as obstacles that a vehicle would have to navigate around. Several miles to the south revealed an outline of a campground, which could barely be distinguished from the barren desert floor. The agent strained his eyes to gain a better view. Could this be the campground Frandsen had described? No campers could be observed in this desolate area. The only signs of civilization were galvanized metal covering over campground tables. From the height of the helicopter, no burial sites were visible. Agent Kidd instructed the photographer in the rear helicopter to take photos of the area.

Reviewing a map in the copter, the agent confirmed that this was the Afton Canyon Campground, listed at 4.7 miles from the freeway. The agent had a hunch that this must be the right site. The basis for his gut reaction was the blue-roofed building they had discovered, which was very distinctive, especially when one was driving toward Vegas at night. In the dark, one could easily fixate on this structure when driving through this isolated part of the desert. This building could be particularly noticeable from a distance, since it had lights shining on the roof displaying the internet sign. No other similar buildings were visible. At night, this could act as a beacon for weary drivers fighting to stay awake. That may explain why Frandsen used it as a land marker when he was describing the site to the agents.

The Afton Canyon Campground was the perfect place to bury bodies. The remoteness and the hilly terrain provided the cover for any type of nefarious activity. Few people would ever have an urge or need to visit this rustic remote campground in the shadow of a busy interstate freeway several ridges over.

Because of its inaccessibility, the question was, would a FBI supervisor give the green light to supply the resources necessary to meticulously search the area for possible gravesites? The field agents realized they didn't have much to justify such an operation. After extensive discussion and consideration, the FBI supervisors agreed to send a team of agents and technicians to conduct the search at the Afton Canyon Campground.

Instead of helicopters, this time the agents traveled by way of undercover cars and vans. It was September 20th, a day the agents knew would be a scorcher in the high desert. Early that morning they sped through the community of Barstow without stopping to soak in its old Western spirit. Continuing on I-15 for several miles, the agents were focused on any structure having a blue roof. Halfway up the freeway to Baker they noticed, in the early morning sun, the mirage of what appeared to be a building with a blue roof on the left side of the freeway.

As they drove closer, the dot-com sign on the top became discernible. In the first car, an excited utterance could be heard over the radio: "That's it, we have arrived!" This message was relayed to the other vehicles as a signal for them to turn off. All the vehicles maneuvered to the right and exited the freeway, where they came to a stop sign. There they were greeted by a sign saying 'Afton Canyon Campground' with an arrow pointing to the right.

Even though Frandsen may not have known the name of the campground, his description so far seemed to be accurate. The right side of the freeway was devoid of any stores or houses. Totally desolate would be a way to describe the terrain. There were no buildings, no trees, and most of all, no signs of civilization. The agents continued to drive down the curvy dirt road, which had to be negotiated with extreme caution. The potholes and gigantic boulders protruded from the roadbed, which could be best be described as an obstacle course more than a roadway. As they descended into a canyon below, giant cliffs lined both sides of the road, releasing rocks to roll down onto the road. Cautiously veered around a hillside, they were confronted by an official Bureau Land Management (BLM) sign declaring this to be Afton Canyon Campground.

They gingerly drove into the campground and directly in front of them was a large plywood sign elucidating the rules of the campground. As the agents surveyed the campground for human life, and seeing none, they wondered why there were all these rules when there was no one around to obey them. The rules specified that a fee collection was set up on the honor system. The procedure was spelled out in detail: first the camper must select a campsite, write down the number on an envelope, and return it to the deposit box. Place the exact cash in an envelope and drop it into a large steel container buried in the ground with layers of concrete.

The agents wondered how many campers actually followed the ‘honor system’ by dropping their money into the fee box. First, it was hard to imagine any camper in their right mind wanting to camp in this godforsaken place. Secondly, there was no ranger or camp director who would be around to enforce the honor system for paying fees.

Earlier, Frandsen had described to the agents that near the entrance to the campground was a large sign, followed by a small outhouse on the central dirt road that weaved its way back to the various campsites. When the agents slowly drove down the main road, they saw a little building to their left that could be the structure Frandsen was referring to. He further mentioned that the campsite they used was at the far end. They continued driving until they reached an area where there was a circle around a large brushy area. It could be compared to a suburban cul-de-sac, except there were no houses or residents.

Then the agents slowly pulled up to the empty campsite. They exited their vehicles and stretched their legs, taking in the ambiance surrounding them. Agent Kelly Dempsey, during the interrogation of the suspect, Frandsen, tried to persuade him to reveal any facts regarding the burial site. As she surveyed the landscape, she tried to remember some detail that might jog her memory as to any clue. No obvious signs jumped out at her indicating where the bodies might be buried in or around this campground. She had to adjust her thinking, since the bodies would have been buried ten months earlier. While standing there she could feel the hot dry winds blowing through her red hair. All those months of howling wind undoubtedly had blown sand and debris over any gravesites that may have existed.

All day the team of FBI agents scoured the entire campground. In order to meticulously search the campground, the supervising agent lined all the agents up in a row at the entrance. He had everyone spaced out at arm's length and then in unison cross the desert floor of the campground, concentrating on the ground they were walking on. After several passes, anyone viewing this moving wave of humanity wouldn't mistake this for a precision drill team. Everyone fastidiously did their jobs, examining every square foot of sand, gravel, and dirt. No signs of a gravesite were visible. Throughout the day, expectations had been raised when something unusual was uncovered, only to have their hopes dashed by realizing that the items discovered were merely trash, or the activities of the wildlife that called this land their home.

The September sun beat down on the searchers, eventually sapping their energy. A panoramic view revealed not one tree anywhere in sight to provide an ounce of shade. As the day progressed, the agents and technical staff were exhausted from the penetrating heat and relentless wind. All the agents had to show for their perseverance was absolutely zero or zilch. With all the negative reporting from the participants, Agent Dempsey had to reassess the entire operation. Had she misjudged what suspect Frandsen had told her? Had she been suckered by an arrestee who would say anything to curry favor with his interrogators? Could all of this be nothing more than looking for the pot of gold at the end of the rainbow?

She kept thinking how convincing Frandsen seemed during the entire interview. Could she take a different approach, one which might be more productive? Everyone agreed that further searching wouldn't uncover anything new, since they had marched over every square inch of the campground more than once. Then someone suggested the possibility of using a "cadaver dog."

These types of dogs are trained to detect the slightest smell of a dead body. The main difficulty with these dogs is the fact they don't always distinguish the difference between dead animals from dead human beings. This area of the desert was littered with dead wild animals. One could spend hours digging up the remains of dead rabbits that had been devoured by coyotes.

The supervising agent could see that his only hope of convincing the team to return for another day was if they tried using a cadaver dog early in the morning, when the wind was still and smells more detectable. With that news, it was agreed to continue the search for one more day.

(On the following graphic page are two of the exhibits showing the turnoff in the desert to the Afton Canyon Campground.)

GRAVE SITE

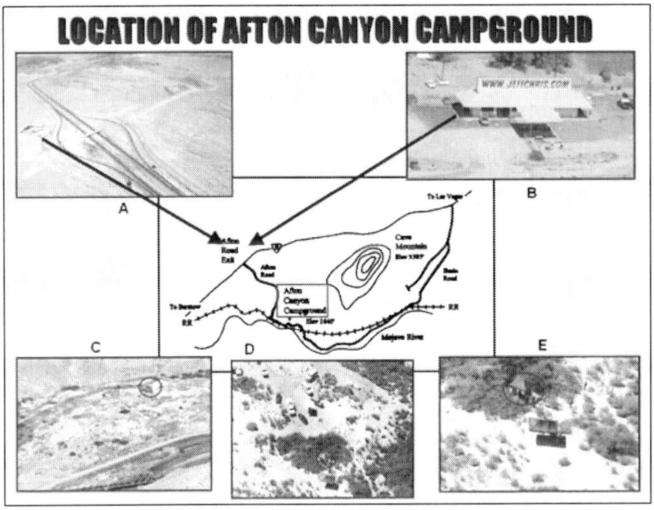
LOCATION OF AFTON CANYON CAMPGROUND
A
B
To Las Vegas
Afton Road Exit
Afton Road
Cave Mountain
Afton Canyon Campground
To Barstow
RR
RR
Mojave River
C
D
E

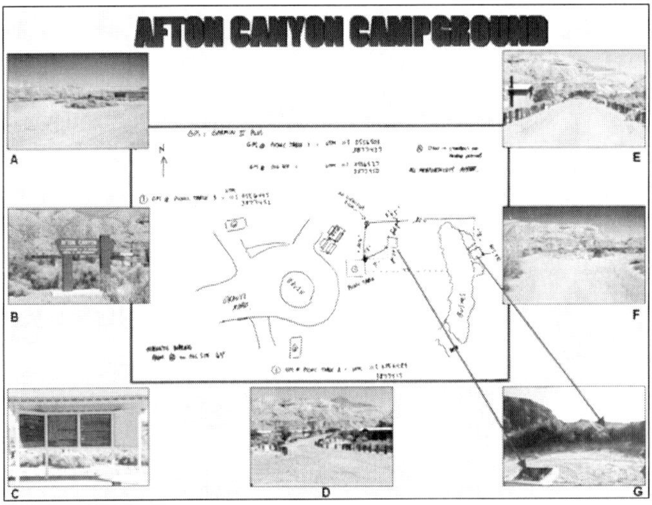
AFTON CANYON CAMPGROUND
A
B
C
D
E
F
G

CHAPTER 3—BRING ON THE CADAVER DOG

The next morning, the cadaver dog arrived early at the campground. At that hour, without the blistering heat and pounding wind, the desert projected the impression of a peaceful site. The dog wandered from one campsite to another, sniffing everything in sight. Not everyone was convinced the cadaver dog was as beneficial as animal lovers make them out to be. Some place these dogs in the same category as psychics when it comes to locating dead bodies. To the pure scientist, it is hard to prove the validity of a dog's reactions. Nonetheless, when the pressure is on in finding a murder victim, law enforcement is willing to try anything to illustrate their commitment in locating a victim or victims, even if there is some question as to its effectiveness.

The victims' Israeli mothers were committed to finding their sons, dead or alive. They believed they had received the runaround from law enforcement and that no one cared about their missing sons. They couldn't get LAPD to investigate, as the mothers couldn't prove that their sons were missing from the City of Los Angeles. Likewise, when they contacted the Las Vegas Metropolitan Police, they received no real assistance since they couldn't prove their sons had gone missing from that jurisdiction. No one would investigate how and when their sons went missing. Their only hope was that the FBI, who indicated that they would look into the matter but couldn't offer any promises.

The FBI agents recognized how much the two mothers were counting on them to solve the mystery of what happened to their sons. Also, the government of Israel, as well as the Israeli news media, was vitally interested in the USA's efforts in finding the two missing young Israeli men. Since so many eyes were focused on the FBI agents, they felt the subliminal pressure to do whatever was necessary to explore all possibilities, no matter how slim the chances of success.

Agent Dempsey's immediate concern wasn't the merits and reliability of cadaver dogs. Her relief was just having an additional day for the team to scour the area for any possible clues. The cadaver dog, without any prodding, headed in the direction of the campsites at the end of the main road, which curves around in a circle. The dog's nose was pointed downward, sniffing every pebble and twig, constantly turning from side to side to check everything out. The dog and his handler wandered into the last campsite. The dog didn't seem to be content in staying near campfire pits or concrete slabs used for tents. Cautiously, the dog worked his way around the brushy area that walled in the campsite. Finally, it managed to maneuver to the backside of the campsite. The dog hesitated for a moment and began to stick his noise in a sandy area, and then he began pawing in the soil as though he was looking for a bone.

Someone brought a shovel over and started to dig in the soft sand. Nothing seemed to indicate the existence of a gravesite. The search team in the area believed the dog could have smelled some jackrabbit droppings. The agents were disappointed and ready to move on.

The small hole they had scooped out revealed nothing of interest except, to the left side, a dull gray object that could barely be seen. One agent's curiosity was aroused, so he continued to use the shovel and dig under the gray object and threw the shovel full of sand into a pile to the side. It wasn't a piece of clothing or anything important; after a closer examination it turned out to be a disappointing piece of old duct tape.

No one seemed excited about the duct tape, since it was commonly utilized by campers to fix torn tents or patch leaky water jugs. Up to this point, the agents were frustrated at not finding anything of value. One of the technicians grabbed a rod poker, which is a device searchers use to determine the firmness of the soil. He pushed the poker into the soil where the dog had been sniffing. The strange reaction was the poker easily pushed into the sand. Someone said, "Keep digging," as though the softness of the sand was something of importance.

They started to dig a larger hole. The technician who was doing the digging found that it was easier to dig on the right side, since no roots from the brush impeded the scooping out of the soil. When the shovel was thrust into the hole on the left side, the blade struck several knotty roots from the sagebrush on that side of the hole. It seemed strange that the digging was easier in the one spot and harder in the other.

After several more scoops with the shovel, it became apparent the roots of the adjacent brush had been cut or severed along an imaginary line. They started digging in earnest. The soil seemed to be unusually soft sand in this one particular area. What did this mean? Could it be something important, or was it merely a place where some camper had buried hot charcoal or dug a hole to dump their trash?

Any homicide detective knows that most killers who bury their victims use shallow graves that generally are covered with less than a foot of soil. This hole was deeper than that. Most killers are in a hurry to get rid of the body before being seen. As a result, they only dig deep enough to cover the body with a layer of soil so it isn't visible to a passerby. When a body is placed in such a shallow grave, in the desert or mountains, the wild animals living in the area, such as coyotes, can smell the dead body and immediately uncover the corpse. The wildlife doesn't have any reverence for dead human beings. To them it is just an easy meal ticket. Most animals will pull apart the body and drag the larger pieces of the corpse to a safe place where they can devour it without having to share it with other predators. Within a short time, the only parts of a corpse remaining are the skull, pelvic bones, or possibly a rib cage.

Another reason that most graves are so shallow is that the killer will often bury a body in a sandy creek bed. Initially, the loose sand on top is easy to dig through. However, they quickly discover that below the soft top soil layer they encounter big boulders that make it impossible to dig a grave any deeper. Out of necessity, a planned deep grave ends up as a shallow hole.

Neophyte gravediggers quickly learn that when they dump a body in the grave they also end up with a pile of leftover dirt. The killer generally takes this extra soil and makes a mound over the buried body. The idea is that over time the soil will settle down evenly. In reality, it is often this large mound of extra dirt that attracts the attention of passersby. Often curiosity is enough for someone to start kicking away the dirt and uncovering a body. The agents didn't see any typical signs of any type of grave, since there was no mound of dirt nor was there any indentation of a shallow grave.

The agents continued to dig deeper and deeper. Every shovel full of soft sand seemed to create more excitement, hoping that they were on to something. Could this be what they were looking for? Or was this just another disappointment?

Emotions were mixed. Should they hurry up and determine what this all meant, or should they consider this a crime scene and carefully document every step they took and examine carefully every shovel-full of dirt?

After digging several more feet, they came upon something hard. They scraped the shovel against it and noticed it to appear to be a shoe. This was a mixed signal. This could mean that someone had buried a bunch of old clothing, including worn-out shoes, in a hole just to get rid of their old trash. They quickly discovered the shoe wasn't all by itself. Attached to the shoe appeared to be a human leg. At that point, the brakes went on and everything switched to a crime-scene mode in which preserving evidence was paramount.

(On the following graphic page are exhibits of the location where the grave was found.)

Graphic 4

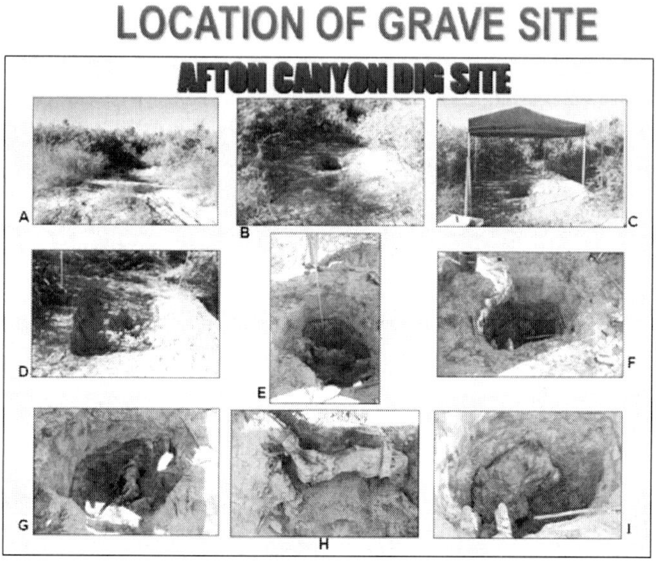
LOCATION OF GRAVE SITE
AFTON CANYON DIG SITE
A
B
C
D
E
F
G
H
I

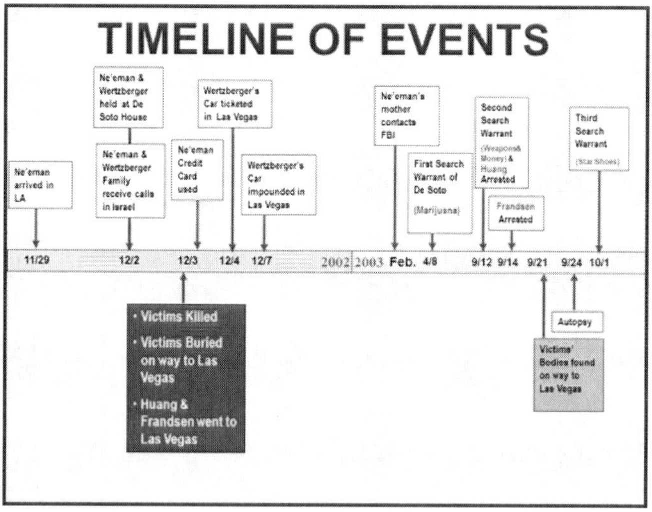
TIMELINE OF EVENTS
Ne'eman arrived in LA
Ne'eman & Wertzberger held at De Soto House
Ne'eman & Wertzberger Family receive calls in Israel
Ne'eman Credit Card used
Wertzberger's Car ticketed in Las Vegas
Wertzberger's Car impounded in Las Vegas
Ne'eman's mother contacts FBI
First Search Warrant of De Soto (Marijuana)
Second Search Warrant (Weapons& Money) & Huang Arrested
Frandsen Arrested
Third Search Warrant (Star Shoes)
11/29
12/2
12/3
12/4
12/7
2002
2003
Feb.
4/8
9/12
9/14
9/21
9/24
10/1
• Victims Killed
• Victims Buried on way to Las Vegas
• Huang & Frandsen went to Las Vegas
Autopsy
Victims' Bodies found on way to Las Vegas

CHAPTER 4—VICTIMS' MOTHERS WANT SOMETHING DONE

The two young men just seemed to vanish into thin air. Both were 24 years old and in the prime of their lives. Handsome and virile would be an accurate description of them. No one knew their whereabouts. Could they have run off on a new life adventure? Did they meet a couple of young sexy hotties who played them for fools? Or were they merely leisurely hitchhiking across the country, enjoying all the sites? On the sinister side, could something bad or evil have happened to these two young, fun-loving men from Israel?

Both were close to their families and in constant contact with them. It was at the end of November 2002, when the phone calls were more sporadic since the young men were moving around between Los Angeles and Vegas.

Yet what triggered Ben and Adar's parents' anxiety was when they received a peculiar phone call from a woman who said their sons would soon be sending them a surprise. This occurred around 8:00 a.m. December 3, 2002, Israeli time. The woman inquired if she had their correct mailing address. She recited the address and they confirmed it was correct. Both families became suspicious about such an odd phone call from a stranger. They consulted each other and agreed something was amiss. Immediately they called their sons' cellphones without receiving any response. They repeatedly called, but neither of their sons answered the calls, which then transferred over to their voice mail.

Days went by without their sons calling back. Where could they be and what were they doing? Since the parents were thousands of miles away in Israel, they had to contact their sons' friends to check on their whereabouts. One of Ben Wertzberger friends told Ben's parents that Ben was in Los Angeles to pay off a phone bill and afterwards was headed back to Las Vegas.

Adar Ne'eman's parents knew their son had left Israel to visit New York for several weeks, after which he flew to sunny Southern California to visit his longtime friend Ben Wertzberger. Several years earlier, Ben had come to Los Angeles in hopes of making it big as a disc jockey (DJ) in the Hollywood clubs. During the years in L.A., he had lived with various friends. Ben, in July 2002, lived in a house on De Soto Avenue in the San Fernando Valley.

Adar's mother, Sylvie Ne'eman, sensed something was wrong. She and her husband operated an Israeli dance troupe that often toured Europe. A mother's instincts generally prove to be correct. When things didn't add up, she wanted things checked out. She remembered that they had set up separate credit cards for Adar to travel freely in the USA. She contacted the credit card companies to see what activities had occurred on his credit cards. To her surprise, the Israeli Card had been used several times on December 3rd in Las Vegas at a clothing store and at an Outback Restaurant. The American Express card had been used in an attempt to purchase $8,000 worth of computers at the Best Buy store in Vegas. As a mother, she knew all of this credit card activity was out of character for her son.

As days turned into weeks without any communication, Ben Wertzberger's parents received information from one of Ben's friends that his car, a Chevrolet Cavalier, had been impounded in Las Vegas. What did all this mean? The two sets of parents needed someone to sort it all out. Phone calls to the Las Vegas Metropolitan Police weren't going anywhere. The police stated that they have 17,000 missing persons reports per year so there wasn't much they could do. Furthermore, there was no proof that the two young men had ever arrived in Vegas. The fact that Wertzberger's car was found in Vegas didn't prove he had driven it there. The car could have been stolen and driven to Vegas by someone else. The men's families were at a disadvantage, since neither lived nearby so they couldn't personally check on their sons.

The mothers didn't know where to turn for help. They had never been in such a helpless situation of not knowing the whereabouts of their children. Finally, out of desperation, the families contacted a private investigator to survey the situation. First off, the private investigator obtained Adar's credit card receipts. The December activity indicated that Adar or someone else had used his credit card on two occasions on December 3rd in Las Vegas.

The private investigator went to the Catwalk, in Las Vegas, and spoke to the sales clerk who had sold clothing to two guys who had used Adar's credit card. The PI showed a single photo of each of the young men and asked the clerk if these were the guys who bought the clothes. The sales clerk viewed a photo of Adar. Slowly shaking her head, she said she had never seen Adar. Then she looked at the photo of Ben Wertzberger. She spent several moments viewing it and then turned her head and said that the photo of Wertzberger looked like one of the guys who bought the clothes. She remembered that person had dark curly hair.

Then the PI went to the Vegas automobile impound lot and checked out Wertzberger's car. He noticed large pieces of luggage that appeared to belong to the two boys. He made arrangements to have the car transported back to Los Angeles.

The PI contacted the media to show them photos of both Ben and Adar. Eventually, the media became interested and ran several stories on the two missing Israeli men. The result was that a bartender in the little community of Round Mountain, some 80 miles northeast of Las Vegas, claimed he had seen the two Israeli men on the 1st of December. Photos were shown around the Round Mountain community of 500, and a motel operator was certain both men had stayed at her place.

This all became baffling to the parents because it didn't add up. How could the men travel to this remote area when Ben's car had been impounded in the center of Vegas? How could they have traveled to Round Mountain? The Metropolitan Police sent an investigator to Round Mountain, where he was able to verify that the men had been there.

By this time, the Israeli mothers flew to Los Angeles and instantly met with the Private Investigator to try and sort this all out. They followed the PI to Las Vegas and personally talked to the merchants where Adar's credit card had been used. The mothers saw first-hand that people were identifying their sons as being in Vegas. They then met with the Las Vegas Metropolitan investigator, who assured them their sons were fine and just wanted to get away from their mothers. These comments were not well received by either of the concerned Israeli mothers; they were infuriated at such a statement.

The PI hadn't uncovered any useable leads in finding the two young men, and the PI bills were piling up for the families. What should the mothers do? Where could they turn for help?

CHAPTER 5—MISSING PERSON DILEMMA

The dilemma for the victims' mothers was that the Las Vegas Metropolitan Police took the position their sons were not 'Missing Persons' but kids wanting to be free of their parents. When the mothers contacted LAPD, they hit another brick wall. LAPD claimed there was no proof the men were ever missing from Los Angeles. Their contention was the young men's friends said they had left for Las Vegas and that was the proper agency to look for them. Years ago, this would have been called a 'Catch 22' situation. That meant no law enforcement agency would pursue an investigation to find their sons.

As the months went by and still no contact from their sons, the mothers' frustration grew. Desperation set in, and they thought it was just the two mothers against the world. Their only option was to find another private investigation agency that would take a fresh look and thoroughly review all the sightings. This time the new PI concentrated on Ben Wertzberger living in Los Angeles. This proved to be very interesting, and at the same time provided information that no parent wants to hear about their son. The PI learned that Ben Wertzberger had really been the caretaker of a marijuana cultivating business. He had been associating with some unsavory characters.

This information was disturbing but helped fit the pieces of the puzzle together. This PI knew the Round Mountain, Nevada, sightings didn't add up. He sent an investigator directly to Round Mountain, who made more inquiries at the motel where the men allegedly stayed. This time he got the names of the men from the registration card. The names were Eled Leshon and Roi Yegger. When the names were checked out through Israeli authorities, it was learned that both men had been traveling through the West and happened to be alive and well in San Francisco.

What did all this mean? All the so-called sightings of both Ben and Adar, in the Las Vegas area, became suspicious and could be a misidentification. But what was needed was a thorough investigation by law enforcement authorities. The mothers were very instrumental in obtaining media coverage about their missing sons in Israel. It had generated so much interest that an Israeli TV documentary was being made, showing the mothers' extreme efforts to find out what happened to their sons in the USA.

In February 2003, the mothers flew to L.A. to locate someone to conduct an investigation. They had visited the Israeli consulate and were told that when the consulate had problems about crimes committed against an Israeli, they had a person in the US State Department who they would contact. That person would contact someone with the FBI, who would look into the matter.

The mothers had sought to encourage the FBI to become interested, but they were told that Missing Persons cases are to be referred to the local law enforcement agency where the missing person disappeared. These two Israeli mothers had already learned how to use the media to put pressure on authorities. The mothers knew how to generate interest, and it all began by going to a local Staples store. They purchased several large poster boards and several colorful Marks-A-Lots pens. They went to work on making posters saying "Where is Ben?" or "Bring Adar & Ben Back."

Even though the posters weren't works of, they were large and colorful enough to create attention. Next was where to display the posters. As every real estate agent knows, the key word is "location," "location," and "location." So both mothers stood in front of the FBI West Coast Headquarters on the corner of Veteran Ave. and Wilshire Blvd. in Westwood (part of West LA) holding up the signs to all passing cars. For several days, the mothers were out holding up their posters. Anyone in the FBI working in the high-rise building had a bird's eye view of the two mothers waving their posters to anyone in sight.

Somehow one day they were asked to meet with FBI Senior Special Agent Mark Williams about their sons' disappearance. The meeting started out with the disclaimer the FBI didn't work missing persons cases like their sons'. The proper agency was the local authorities from where they went missing. These Israeli mothers politely responded that neither Los Angeles nor Las Vegas police would conduct an investigation since the mothers couldn't prove where their sons had disappeared from.

Agent Williams listened to the mothers and he quickly sensed the hopelessness they felt that no one in law enforcement would undertake a missing person investigation. It had now been three months since the mothers had heard from their sons. Agent Williams got the feeling he was the end of the line for these mothers. What harm could it do to have one of the FBI agents make a few phone calls and track down the whereabouts of these two young men?

CHAPTER 6—THE LIFE OF BEN WERTZBERGER

The missing young men, Ben Wertzberger and Adar Ne'eman, grew up together in the same small town in Israel. Their lives paralleled each other growing up from childhood to teenage years and eventually completing their military service together. Ben loved music, to the point he had a fixation for it. He knew all the words to every song on the radio and literally knew every aspect of a recording artist's background. For fun, he would play music at parties, and he relished playing the role of disc jockey. Ben was truly an overachiever and wanted to be the best at whatever he did. He studied the careers of successful DJs to understand the dynamics of the business and their secrets of success.

In order to make it to the top, he had to travel to Southern California. There he could work with professional DJs to better understand sound systems and learn how to operate all the high-tech equipment. To Ben this was all necessary in order to qualify for high-paying jobs in exclusive nightclubs.

After saving up his money, he had enough to fly to Los Angeles to pursue his dream. Upon his arrival, Ben rented a room at a home in Porter Ranch, which is at the north end of Los Angeles. Because of its remote location it was difficult for him to travel to any DJ jobs. He soon realized that he needed to be more centralized for the DJ jobs, so he moved to the Hollywood area. Everyone would agree Ben had pleasing social skills and could be the life of the party. Within a short time, women noticed Ben, who could be described as easy on the eyes, energetic, and some might say a bit of a hustler. His female following was good for his ego, but not so good for his wallet. He would have preferred moving in more affluent circles, but the reality was that he made next to nothing from his DJ jobs.

In order to improve his source of revenue, he took up selling artwork to homeowners. A group of Israeli guys had latched onto the business venture of selling reproduction art from door to door. This might seem like a futile waste of time; however, for good talkers it could be quite lucrative. Of course, you might have to fabricate the sales pitch a little bit by claiming that you actually painted the canvas. Often a homeowner thought they were buying from a struggling artist whose works would be worth thousands of dollars someday. However, the sellers were truly 'struggling' but they weren't real 'artists.'

Ben's smile and low-key sales approach allowed him to make a living at this business. In due course he bought a well-used Chevy Cavalier, which would never be considered a 'Chick Mobile' but was the best he could afford. Now, with a set of four wheels he was able to attract the attention of Krista Autry (Pseudonym), who fell for his exuberant charm. She thought Ben's passion for music was magical. Ben and Krista had a unique chemistry. Ben wanted the relationship with Krista to grow, but first he needed to be able to put a roof over their heads. Through a friend, he heard about a caretaker's job at a house in Canoga Park, which would furnish him free rent. All he had to do was care for the marijuana plants being cultivated in two of the back bedrooms.

It all seemed simple enough, since Ben had no objection to using or growing marijuana. His main duty was guarding it from others, watering the plants, and harvesting the marijuana leaves when they were ready. He was pleased with the setup and convinced Krista to move in with him into one of the remaining bedrooms, which could best be described as 'cozy' or 'downright tiny.' Here he lived rent-free, permitting him to save up his money, and the hours were flexible, so he could book more DJ jobs. But after three months, Krista didn't like the confining conditions of living in a marijuana house, so she moved out. That made Ben rethink what he was trying to accomplish.

He had friends in Las Vegas who regularly told stories of how easy it was to get DJ jobs there with all the hotels and casinos. Since his opportunities were dwindling in Los Angeles, Ben listened to how the grass was greener in Vegas. One day he drove his old car up there to check things out and quickly came to the conclusion that his prospects were much brighter in Vegas with all the lights. He got situated in Las Vegas and started making contacts. Then, at the end of November, he returned to Los Angeles to finish up one of his remaining DJ jobs in downtown L.A.

At the same time, he received word that his dear friend, Adar Ne'eman, was flying in from New York to visit him. Ben worked out arrangements so he could spend a couple of nights at one of his friends' places while he waited for Adar to arrive for his visit. When Adar arrived, Ben picked him up at the airport. Ben enjoyed playing the role of the tour guide driving Adar through the renowned streets of Beverly Hills and down Hollywood Blvd catching a glimpse of tinsel town's glitz. The next day they headed for the beaches in Santa Monica and Venice. Adar's eyes were fixated on the pretty girls prancing along the strand in their short shorts.

Ben needed to reimburse several people for money he had borrowed from when he needed money to pay his phone bills. As soon as he made contact with everyone, he and Adar would drive to Vegas, where he had rented an apartment with two other guys.

CHAPTER 7—THE PERFECT LIFE OF SHANE

A young man on top of the world would be a good way of defining Shane Huang who could be characterized as good looking, incredibly bright, highly personable guy from an affluent family. Having a BS degree in business management from the University of California at Davis allowed him to gain a high-paying job in the Los Angeles financial district. After several years in the business world he realized the road to the top required a Masters of Business Administration (MBA) degree. In order to achieve his goal, he enrolled in the prestigious UCLA Anderson School of Business. An MBA degree would guarantee him success in whatever business venture he undertook.

Even with a busy work schedule and the demanding graduate classes, Shane lived the good life in Venice, California, which is a beach community where young professionals congregate to play and live. This neighborhood was patterned after the City of Venice, Italy, with all the canals and bridges. Good ideas don't always reach the expectations they are set out to emulate. The California version of Venice lacks the romance and allure of the real Venice. This one has a Bohemian flavor to it, with the rich and poor living side by side. Living on the beach in So. Cal. has its advantages. There is an endless supply of attractive young women flaunting their perfectly suntanned bodies in skimpy bikinis. They can be classified as true 'California Girls' as made famous by the 'Beach Boys.'

Shane, the true entrepreneur, watched for opportunities to make fast money. He leased a four-bedroom house on De Soto Avenue in Canoga Park, located in the westerly portion of the San Fernando Valley. A fun-loving graduate student wouldn't find this an appealing place to live. This area could best described as a bedroom community made up of cookie-cutter tract homes from the early 50s. Shane had the business savvy to transform this dilapidated house into a money maker.

The main purpose of this Canoga Park house was for clandestinely growing, cultivating, and harvesting marijuana for sale. Back in 2002, a person in California could possess and cultivate their own marijuana for medical purposes, as long as a doctor prescribes it. (Not until 2016, were the marijuana laws in Califnornia drasticaly changed.) Shane, however, was not even going to concoct a notion that this marijuana was for medical purposes. Shane's objective was simple: he envisioned large profits from a cash business devoid of any income taxes.

He gutted two bedrooms to accommodate a hydro watering and lighting system. Then he installed 75 large containers all planted with marijuana bushes. To prevent law enforcement from ever discovering these growing rooms, a false wall was built across the hallway. A full-length mirror covered the fake wall with a petite door behind the mirror, which provided access to the workers in order to enter the growing rooms. Anyone walking into the house wouldn't notice that the two growing rooms were hidden behind the fake wall.

Shane thought fixing up the house might cause the neighbors to become suspicious. He wanted it to retain its deteriorating condition. One of the unique features of this nondescript tract house was its color. The prior owner had painted it a light pink, which had faded over time. Initially it seemed a little strange for single guy to be living in a pink house. Fortunately, Shane and the other guys didn't pay any attention to the color of the house and definitely lacked any interest in sprucing up the dingy stucco and wood-rot exterior. After leasing the house, he didn't spend any time or money redecorating the interior of the house. Nobody wasted time installing new shelf paper in the cupboards. Redoing the window treatments was not high on his priority list and in fact not even contemplated. The growing room windows had been totally covered in such a way as to not create suspicion. Even the wall-to wall tattered carpet was a shade of pink.

The odd color combinations didn't phase the guys in turning the front rooms into a bachelor pad with no frills. At one time the guys had a portable hot tub in the living room. Most visitors were surprised to walk in the front door and be greeted by a three-foot-high hot tub next to the fireplace in the living room. Even in causal San Fernando Valley, hot tubs in living rooms weren't standard décor in most households.

Because of the placement of the house on the lot, the occupants had total privacy from the outside world. Even though this tract house didn't have the ambiance that the Venice Beach house possessed, it did have features that made it the perfect place to socialize with ultimate privacy. When Ben was living and working in the pink house, Shane had a secure feeling. Ben was reliable and made sure everything was done according to Shane's wishes. Shane would have liked Ben to continue to live there. However, when Ben announced that he would be moving out so he could further his career in Vegas, Shane wasn't pleased that he was losing such a trustworthy caretaker.

Phone bills can be challenging among roommates, and that was no different from the situation in the pink house. Ben acknowledged that he owed money and agreed to pay his part as soon as he received money from one of his DJ jobs. The settling of the phone bill would allow Shane and Ben to have an amicable parting of ways.

(On the following page are the exhibits photo boards showing the house were the marijuana was grown as well as where the victims were held.)

Graphic 5

HOUSE- CRIME SCENE

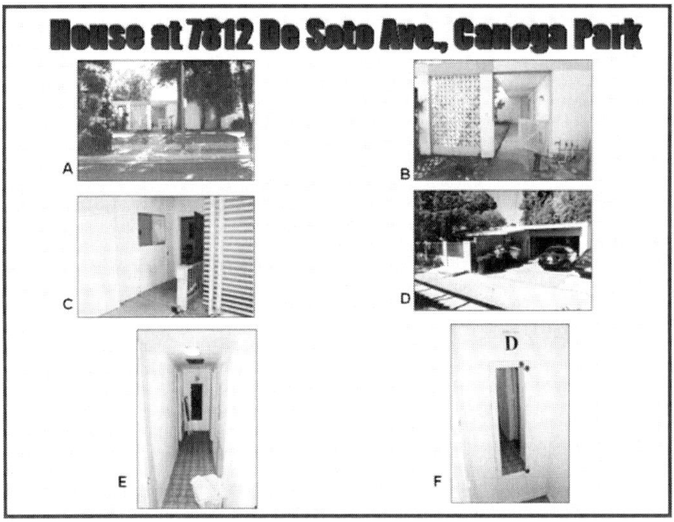

CHAPTER 8—CATCHING BURGLARS

Shortly after Ben had moved out of the pink house, someone broke in and seized all the useable marijuana. This brazen theft surprised and shocked Shane. Who could sneak into his place in the dead of night and steal his property? Shane's mind operated like a calculator. He visualized the world in dollars and cents and quickly assessed the loss at a total of over $5,000. As a shrewd businessman, Shane didn't like losing money. Instantly, Shane tried to analyze who could have done this to him. Who did he know that fit the definition of a thief? He couldn't fathom how anyone would challenge him, a candidate who shortly would have an MBA degree. Shane prided himself in doing a risk-management analysis of all his business decisions.

Since his marijuana plants had been ripped off, who could Shane enlist for help to catch the thief? Shane couldn't make a police report about the theft. When conducting an illegal business, such as cultivating marijuana, the reliance of having the services of the police and courts wasn't an option for him.

He assembled his closest circle of friends to seek their advice in figuring out who the culprit could be. No one knew for sure, but someone mentioned Ben's name. Some were suspicious, since he had just moved out and shortly thereafter the theft occurred.

Shane had his friend Jamil Khachatouian (Pseudonym), known as the "Russian Guy," come by to discuss possible suspects. Another visitor was Joe Pierson

(Pseudonym), known as the "Plumber Guy," who was a whiz when it came to irrigation systems. He also contacted his longtime friend, Ben Frandsen, who greatly admired Shane. Frandsen had no interest in the marijuana-growing business. He aspired to be a writer, all though no big break had come along. Frandsen lived downtown Los Angeles in the Chinatown area with his roommate Nicolas Tuttle (Pseudonym).

Shane didn't know for sure who the culprit could be. His friends surmised that Ben Wertzberger could be the thief. Someone said that Ben had returned to L.A. to pay off some people he owed money to regarding an old phone bill. Shane decided to pursue that notion and drove over to Khachatouian's place in hopes of finding Ben with the phone bill money. Unfortunately, Ben never appeared, and Shane returned to the pink house to check on the security of the dwelling.

Shane slowly drove by the front of the pink house and noticed Ben's car parked next to the curb. Surprised at the situation, Shane drove, unnoticed, to the back alley and parked at the rear of the house. After stepping out of his car, he crept to the rear of the house, peeking through the wooden slats to peer into the backyard. Around the corner, he could make out the figure of a person who resembled Ben near the back window. From his vantage point, he couldn't see clearly. Had Shane caught Ben in the act of breaking in? Shane hastily maneuvered himself so he could enter the backside door and find something to arm himself. Inside the house, Shane reached into a cupboard and removed a yard-long sword. He quietly tiptoed out to the side of the house. He surprised Ben and pointed the sword at him.

A tense situation developed. Shane began accusing Ben of being a burglar. He demanded that Ben explain what he was doing trying to open one of the back windows of the house. Without waiting for an explanation, Shane marched Ben out to Ben's car and ordered the person inside the car to follow them inside the house. That other person was Ben's friend, Adar, who meekly followed the two into the house. Ben and Adar had to be frightened as Shane continued to wave the sword in their faces. They didn't know how to react, but in their minds this would be all straightened out within minutes. Ben and Adar showed no resistance and complied with Shane's demands. Shane shouted at the two guys to sit on the sofa, which they did obediently, so as not to further enrage Shane. Frantically, Shane waved the sword while he methodically made phone calls to his buddies, asking for their assistance. Within minutes, Shane's pals started appearing at the house, one by one. It had the appearance of a fraternity party in which someone forgot to bring the beer.

Ben profusely explained he came by to collect the remaining items that he had left behind when he moved out. By now, Shane had no doubts in his mind that Ben had burglarized his place two days earlier. Even without any eyewitnesses, or evidence, Shane was convinced that Ben had stolen all the marijuana. Shane had made up his mind. The best way to describe his behavior was that of a person experiencing a paranoiac frenzy state.

Adar couldn't figure out how he had become entangled in this mess. Only the week before, he was enjoying the sites of New York. Ben kept reiterating that he only wanted his own belongings and he would be on his way to Vegas. To show his goodwill he had brought $100 to pay off the phone bill he owed. Shane had passed the point of rational thinking. What would it take to pressure Ben to pay him the $5,000, which he considered the value of the stolen marijuana from the burglary?

As the afternoon wore on, so did the stalemate. Shane had called all his associates who were involved in the cultivation business to provide a united front to pressure Ben. The "Russian Guy" was the person who had originally brought Ben and Shane together. Shane relied heavily on his expertise to make the marijuana business a success. The Russian Guy in his own way tried to pressure Ben to come up with the money. Next was the "Plumber Man," who by his nickname was the "fix it man" making sure all the equipment worked properly in growing the marijuana. He tried to come across as a tough guy, demanding that Ben pay what he owed for the loss.

By 3:30 p.m., the last group of friends, Frandsen and Nick Tuttle, arrived at Shane's little gathering of all those with a vested interest. These two guys, Frandsen and Tuttle, had been in the Marine Corps at the same time. Misfits and loners don't accurately describe them. They had known each other since childhood and basically grown up together. Presently they shared an apartment, drifting through life with hopes of helping the poor and oppressed around the world. What could they contribute to Shane's get-together? Frandsen knew Shane and wanted to help him out. When Frandsen arrived at the De Soto address, he had on fatigues and gloves, projecting a rough, threatening image.

By early afternoon, everyone had assembled at the pink house. Shane ranted and raved as Ben and Adar sat terrified on the couch. Shane would wave the sword in Ben's face to appear as threatening as possible. Several times Shane addressed his crowd of supporters, asking if anyone would care if he killed Ben and Adar. As macho as the group tried to be, Nick Tuttle spoke up and stated that he would tell the truth if the police were to ask him. What a strange response. It caught Shane off guard, so he changed the topic. Shane now didn't know the allegiance of his group. Finally, he told his buddies to tie the victims' hands and feet with duct tape.

Somehow this eased the tension and created a more secure environment. Then someone expressed a feeling of hunger. In order not to lose his army of supporters, Shane directed someone to take everyone's order for food. It seemed surreal, taking everyone's order for Subway sandwiches with extra pickles, hold the mayo but extra mustard. This all supported the old axiom that 'an army travels on its stomach.' When they returned with all the sandwiches and potato chips, the mood changed. The food had taken the place of the smoking of a peace pipe, in that, everyone seemed to chill out.

Shortly thereafter, Shane left with Frandsen to drive over to the local Home Depot. There they invested in a shovel and some rope. When they returned, they found someone had passed a joint around for everyone, even the victims, to relieve the stress and mellow out anyone's anxiety. With food and a joint the hostile atmosphere had waned.

Shane continued to made demands for his money as Ben vigorously denied any involvement and explained that he couldn't have done it because he was in Las Vegas when the theft occurred. Shane didn't care about excuses. But how could Shane extract $5,000 from Ben, who didn't have that large amount of money to his name, nor did he have any friends who did? He did not associate with people who would have access to that kind of money. So Shane had to contemplate how to get blood out of a turnip.

(On the following graphic page is the exhibit of the layout of the pink house. Below that is the map that shows where various events occurred.)

Graphic 6

DIAGRAMS & MAP

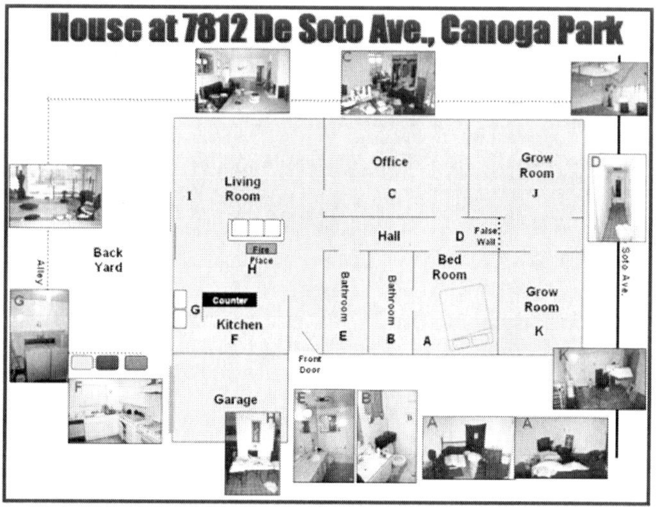

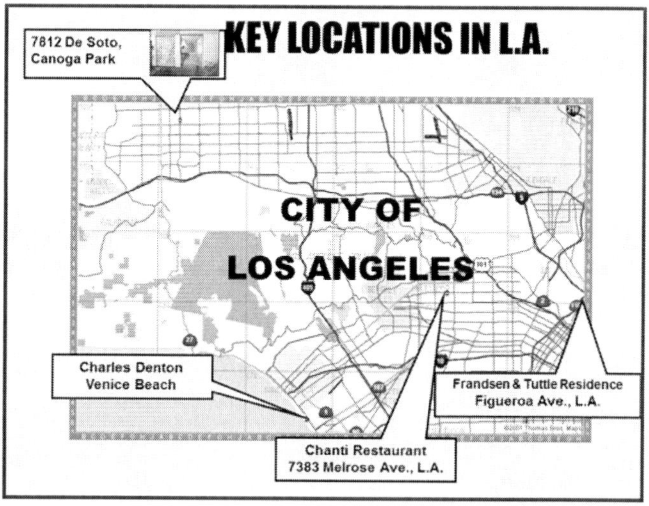

CHAPTER 9—PLAN TO EXTORT PAYMENT

Shane, the businessman, grasped the problem that Ben lacked financial liquidity. Therefore, the negotiations progressed to a different level. Why not have Ben pay off the amount through installment payments? To make this work, Shane would have to trust Ben to make the future payments. Over the past months while Ben lived at the house, Shane learned about Ben's strong family ties to his parents in Israel. Every day, Ben phoned his family and informed them what he was doing. Most of these phone calls painted a picture that he had become incredibly successful.

Shane had an idea, that he would threaten to tell Ben's parents that their son was a "no good thief." Also, Shane would tell his family members the truth that Ben had not become a successful Disc Jockey, as he had claimed. For months, Ben had bragged to his relatives that he only had to work one job since he made so much money. To support his stories he boasted that he had made so much that he had bought a convertible sports car from his earnings.

Shane knew that Ben would do anything to prevent his parents from learning the truth that he had failed at his dream and ended up working in the drug business. In order to ensure that Ben would follow through, Shane needed to know Ben's parents' phone number and address. If Ben provided that, Shane could contact his parents at any time and tell them what a failure he had become. Shane knew that Ben would do anything to prevent his parents from learning the truth about his lack of success. Shane was certain that Ben would be able to pay him by using the installment method. For added measure, Shane demanded that Ben's friend Adar provide his parents' information so he would have additional leverage over the two young men. After obtaining all that personal information from both of them, the situation seemed to be defused. Within minutes, the young men would be released and they would be on their way to Vegas.

Then one of Shane's cronies mentioned the possibility that the young men may not have given accurate information about their parents' addresses. Shane reflected on that likelihood and came to the conclusion that it would be easy enough to verify their family information. Shane said that he would call the numbers and check them out. After some thought he realized his idea would not work since the parents in Israel didn't speak English. He needed someone who spoke their language to verify the information was correct. Shane started thinking what friends he knew who would be willing to help him out to verify the information. Most of his acquaintances would question why the calls were being made.

Then he remembered a gutsy broad he knew by the name of Ora Vodnoy (Pseudonym). She worked at the "Attitude for Men" clothing store on Melrose Blvd., in the Hollywood area. He called her cellphone but didn't receive any answer. Then he tried her work phone and she answered. He briefly explained that he needed her help to make a couple of phone calls. She said, "Well sure why not? You'll have to wait until I'm off work." She indicated that she would be available around 8:30 p.m. If Shane still wanted her to help, all he had to do was call her on her cellphone.

Shane didn't have any other option, so he waited for Ora to finish work. Because of this delay, Shane convinced his friends to stay at the De Soto house to guard Ben and Adar so they couldn't escape while Shane verified the parents' information.

He arranged to meet Ora at the fashionable Chianti's Restaurant across the street from her store. The restaurant is well known for its murky, intimate atmosphere. At 9:00 p.m., Shane and his friend Frandsen met her in one of the back booths. Her curiosity was piqued as to the purpose of her calling people to verify their addresses. She exhibited a quirky personality and had learned early on in life not to ask too many questions. Shane explained that he wanted her to verify two addresses. Shane thought the best way to do this was to say that their sons were sending them a surprise package in a couple of days and that she had to verify she had their correct addresses.

Ora used Shane's phone to place the calls. Shane had purchased a calling card so the phone calls wouldn't be charged to his phone. Ora made the first call to Ben Wertzberger's parents' phone and his father answered. She asked to verify their address, which the father did. Next Ora called Adar Ne'eman's parents' home and spoke with Adar's sister, Rona. Again, she was able to verify the address. At this point, Shane had checked everything out and the victims had been truthful about their parents' addresses. Shane thanked Ora for helping him and then he contacted the bartender to make sure she had sufficient drinks for the rest of the evening.

Shane and Frandsen left Ora drinking and enjoying wine in the Chianti Bar. Then they headed to Venice Beach to meet with Shane's friend, Charles Denton (Pseudonym), who he valued as having good instincts. Monday night football had ended by the time they arrived at his seaside apartment. Shane explained his present situation in which he had caught someone who had burglarized his place and taken about $5,000 worth of his marijuana. There they discussed how to handle the situation. Denton said Shane should teach the thief, Ben, a lesson so he knew that Shane meant business and was a person who should be feared. As they continued to talk, Shane became even angrier that someone he had trusted had stolen from him. Denton then put into words what Shane should do. "Fuck him up and then let him go."

By this time, it was getting late and Shane had made a pivotal decision. Had he arrived at the conclusion that his extortion plan wasn't likely to succeed? Did he fear if he released Ben and Adar that they would go directly to the police and make a kidnapping report? During this time, 10:46 p.m. to 10:59 p.m., Shane made two phone calls: one to Dave Sherwood (Pseudonym), one of his classmates in the UCLA MBA program. The two of them had been assigned a group project due in a couple of days, which had to be completed if they wanted to receive their MBA at the May graduation. They had planned on meeting the next morning to finish the paper.

Shane called Sherwood and explained that an emergency had arisen and he had to leave town but he would meet up with him when he returned. What can be inferred from that statement was that Shane had, at least at that moment, decided that he was going to do something with Ben that would require him to leave Los Angeles, at least for one day.

After leaving Venice Beach, Shane and Frandsen drove up the 405 Freeway to the San Fernando Valley. It was past midnight when Shane called Tuttle to make sure that Ben and Adar hadn't escaped. Around 2:00 a.m., Shane and Frandsen arrived back at the pink house. Tuttle was tired and wanted to return home so he could go to bed. Tuttle asked his roommate, Frandsen, if he wanted to return with him to their apartment near downtown. Frandsen indicated that he wanted to stick with Shane.

Since Frandsen didn't have a car, that meant he would have to spend the night at the pink house. If he would or could have left with Tuttle, his life would have forever been different. His choice to stay with his friend Shane would prove to be the most costly decision of his life.

CHAPTER 10—TIME FOR KILLING

By 2:30 a.m., Nick Tuttle had departed. The four people left in the pink house were Shane and Frandsen, who were holding Ben and Adar, the two Israelis against their will. The victims were immobilized, to some extent, by the use of duct tape bound around their hands and feet.

Shane still wanted to find a way to get Ben to admit to the stealing of the marijuana. His Venice buddy, Charles Denton, told him to fuck up the thief to teach him a lesson. What did this mean? What was he supposed to do in order to 'fuck him up?' Shane grabbed Ben off the couch and started pulling him into the bathroom. Since Ben's extremities were tied up, he had to take baby steps to keep from falling. Shane had to assist by partially dragging Ben into the small bathroom. How could he get him to talk?

Shane shoved Ben's head into the toilet bowl and held his head under the water as Ben struggled to get free. After about 15 seconds he yanked his head out, as Ben gasped for air. Shane held Ben's head up and shouted at him to admit the theft. At that point Ben would confess to anything, but he was so out of breath he couldn't utter a word. Shane interpreted that as defiance and with one swift motion, and with all the force he could muster, smashed Ben's head back into the hard porcelain toilet. Ben's body struggled but the impact made him go rigid. Shane continued to pull his head out and shrieked at him, then immediately pushed it back in.

Adar was still seated on the sofa with his hands and feet tied up. He could hear his dear friend Ben struggling for his life. He had a flashback to when the two of them were in the Israeli armed services together. His training was to help his comrade, even if it meant his own life. Adar abruptly stood up, which caught Frandsen off guard. Adar with all his strength charged for the bathroom to save his Army buddy. Frandsen jumped up and with a karate chop struck Adar's neck with all his force. With a momentary stumble, Adar went down to the floor. As Shane backed out of the bathroom dragging Ben's lifeless body, he could see Adar sprawled on the floor.

Frandsen was holding his hand as if he was in pain, and he was jumping on one foot. Shane glanced down at Adar's body and could see him struggling to get up. With one swift move he took his shod foot and smashed it down on Adar's neck, causing a crackling sound. A gagging noise came from Adar's mouth as he gasped for a breath. At that point, Shane put all his weight on his foot over Adar's neck. Shane continued for several minutes standing on Adar until not even a whimper of life was left.

It was as if a horrendous storm had passed over the De Soto house and suddenly there was an eerie silence. Two dead bodies sprawled on the faded pink carpet. Such promising lives had been snuffed out so swiftly. The killers looked like petrified statutes standing over lifeless corpses. Shane and Frandsen tried to gather their thoughts as they glimpsed at each other with a blank face saying, "Now what do we do?"

Shane's analytical mind went into high gear. He realized the real question was, "How do we get away with murder?" Disposing of the bodies could be easily done. But the challenge would be how it could be done to deflect suspicion from the two of them.

Shane remembered that Ben's car had been parked in front of the pink house. He recalled the backseat contained luggage Ben was transporting to Las Vegas. Shane had the brilliant idea that if they drove Ben's car to Vegas and left it there, the inference would be that the two had disappeared from that town. In order to carry out the plan, they drove Ben's car into the garage and closed the garage door. Next they had to drag the bodies, one by one, through the kitchen and into the garage. Neither one of them had dragged dead bodies before, and they found the dead weight was much heavier than expected. With both of the victims' bodies lying at the rear of Ben's car, they opened the trunk and found more luggage. They rearranged the items in the trunk. Then, one grabbed the feet and the other one grabbed the hands as they struggled to lift the motionless bodies up into the trunk.

Next on the agenda for the 'Plan to Get Away with Murder' included painstakingly cleaning the floors in the living room and bathroom. They made sure there was no sign of a struggle, and any blood or bodily fluids were wiped up and disposed of. Since no knife or gun was used in the killings, the crime scene was cleansed in short order.

By 4:00 a.m., they had completed the sanitizing tasks and packed the two cars. Both Shane and Frandsen grabbed their cellphones and climbed into their respective vehicles. Shane led off in his ink black Mustang with the license plate 2EVIL 2 (LOVE this was illustrated by a heart symbol). DMV advertises personalized license plates are a reflection of the owner's personality. If so, why would a young man want such a license plate? In his Mustang's trunk he had placed rope and a shovel, ready for some heavy digging.

Shane gave Frandsen the job of driving Ben's older car, which had many exhaustive miles on it. Frandsen knew he had to obey every traffic law, since he didn't want to take a chance of being stopped by a highway patrol officer, especially when he had two dead bodies in the trunk. Even the best actor would have difficulty explaining to an officer the reason for transporting two corpses.

All the stress of cleaning the house and moving bodies had created an appetite, so the two decided to take a detour to a Denny's Restaurant for a bite to eat. They pulled in and had no difficulty finding a parking space at that hour. Shane hastily parked and stepped out of his car as Frandsen drove up next to him. Frandsen had never driven a Chevrolet Cavalier. After he turned off the engine, the car lights stayed on, so he started pushing buttons on the dashboard. Then he heard a noise from the rear of the car and turned his head to see that the trunk lid had popped open. In his haste, he had pushed the button that opened the trunk.

Panic set in! He thought he had seen a police patrol car passing by. He nonchalantly walked to the rear of the car and promptly slammed the trunk lid shut. He glanced down on both sides of the trunk to check to see if any clothing had gotten caught in the trunk lid. Did anyone see inside the trunk? They both hurriedly walked away from the car as if nothing had happened. As they got to the Denny's door, they smiled and Frandsen shook his head and softly whispered, "That was a close one."

(On the following graphic page are two exhibits which show photos of Shane's car and the other of Ben's car, which was driven by Frandsen.)

Graphic 7

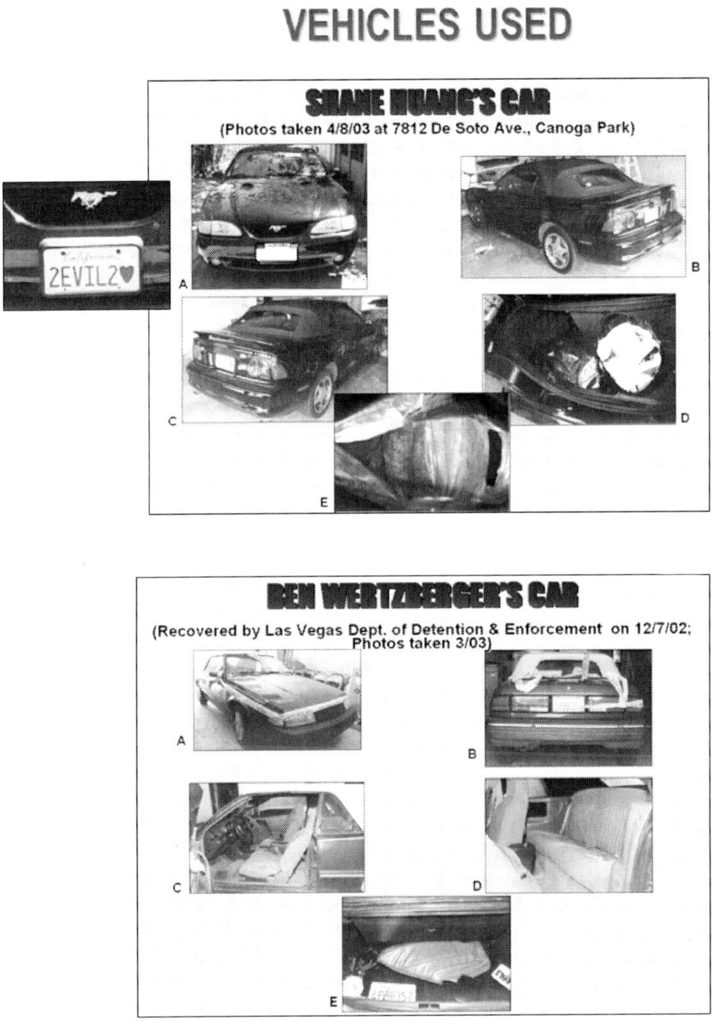
VEHICLES USED
SHANE HUANG'S CAR
(Photos taken 4/8/03 at 7812 De Soto Ave., Canoga Park)
2EVIL2
A
B
C
D
E
BEN WERTZBERGER'S CAR
(Recovered by Las Vegas Dept. of Detention & Enforcement on 12/7/02; Photos taken 3/03)
A
B
C
D
E

CHAPTER 11—ON THE ROAD TO VEGAS

It was shortly after 4:30 a.m. when their mini-caravan of two cars drove out of Denny's and headed for Las Vegas. Using their cellphones, Frandsen and Shane were in constant communication with each other. They proceeded across the San Fernando Valley on the old Ventura Freeway and drove by the Disney Studio proceeding to Eagle Rock. Driving through the west side of Pasadena, they sped by the historic Rose Bowl stadium to the left on the north side. This was familiar to Shane since UCLA played their home games there. Historically, cross-town rival USC had won many national football championships on that gridiron.

There wasn't any traffic at that hour, making it easy to transition onto the 210 Freeway, allowing them to glide through the San Gabriel Valley with ease until they reached the bedroom community of San Dimas, where the freeway lanes narrow down. During rush hour, they would be moving at a snail's pace, but at 5:00 a.m. in the morning they didn't experience any delays. Within a short time, they were merging onto the I-15 freeway making the long, gradual ascent up through the Cajon Pass. Shane's Mustang was purring along as it mounted the challenging mountain pass. However, Frandsen who was driving Ben's old car, could see Shane pulling away from him. He eased his foot off the accelerator, realizing that with all the weight of the luggage and the addition of two dead bodies, the old car could overheat and break down.

During a hot summer day, the side of the freeway is littered with vehicles with their hoods up with steam gushing from the overheated engines. At this early morning hour, a cool breeze swept over the hillside as Frandsen cautiously drove the old Chevy up the hill. The steep grade, plus the heavy load, slowed the vehicle as it struggled to reach the 4189-foot summit. A sense of relief settled over Frandsen as he crested the Cajon Pass, and the two began talking back and forth on their cellphones.

As they arrived at the top of the pass, they made their grand entrance into the vast Mojave Desert, which is known for Edwards Air Force Base. This was where Chuck Yeager traveled faster than the speed of sound in the Bell X-1, and where the Space Shuttles majestically landed on the dry lake bed on numerous occasions. Because of all the miles of barren wasteland, the desert is well known as one of the largest dumping grounds for dead bodies in the country. As they sped past the high desert community of Victorville, civilization thinned out and the lights along the freeway faded to total darkness. Besides the occasional headlights of oncoming traffic, they had entered the world of nothingness for the next 30 miles until they saw the faint glow and light from the desert community of Barstow.

Next on the left is the old Calico Ghost town, which stares down on all the speeding traffic, not revealing its long history of saloon shootings that left a string of dead bodies. East of the ghost town is the Calico Early Man Site where scientists claim they have found man-made tools dating back 200,000 years. The fact that this might be the burial site for the earliest human beings in North America didn't seem to be a consideration in Shane's mind. Without a doubt, this was the perfect area to dispose of dead bodies so they would never be found. They were traveling the infamous 'Road to Vegas,' which would ultimately lead them to the bright lights of Las Vegas.

CHAPTER 12—WHERE TO BURY THE BODIES?

As Shane continued driving down the highway in his Mustang, his mind shifted to the big question: "Where's a good place to bury the victims?" They could pull off on any freeway exit and maneuver down one of the desolate desert roads, and turn off on one of the hundreds of dry riverbeds and find a sheltered area. With no one around for miles, one could leisurely bury a body where no human being would ever find the burial site. Shane had been doing some harried thinking as they caravanned their way to Vegas. In the cobwebs of his memory he recalled attending a Rave concert, somewhere between Barstow and the tiny gas stop town of Baker. The concert location could only be reached by an isolated road that led to a remote campground, hidden by tall hills blocking any view of the Vegas freeway. Shane was desperate to recollect what off-ramp he should take to get to that location. There was a vague memory of a blue-roofed building that marked the exit to take in order to find that campground.

As he traveled eastbound from Barstow, he tried to zero in on the next off-ramp to see if any of the buildings, such as gas stations or restaurants, had a blue roof. Because of the barren landscape, he strained his eyes to penetrate the darkness to try and make out the next beacon of light emerging in the distance. The source of light was like a mirage, and as he sped closer he couldn't recognize any of the buildings. After 30 minutes of searching, he was finally able to make out an older building that had a light blue roof and a dot com sign on top. This jogged his memory and he slowed down his Mustang and pulled over into the right hand lane. As he approached the freeway off-ramp, he veered to the right and exited. Through the rear view mirror, he could see the headlights of the car Frandsen was driving pull over behind him as they both stopped.

Shane could vaguely make out a sign in from of him. Straining his eyes, he could see that the sign read 'Afton Canyon Campground' and pointed to the right. At this point Shane knew he was headed in the right direction. They proceeded southbound on a narrow paved road that within minutes disintegrated into a dirt road peppered with softball-size rocks. On the freeway, they had been cruising at 80 mph and now were crawling along at 10 mph with their cars' undercarriages scraping the loftier rocks as they passed over them. Shane was relieved there was no one around as their headlights cut a path through the desert darkness. They descended a hilly ravine and then rose up to the top and saw a railroad trestle that ran across a dry creek bed. They had traveled over several miles from the so called Road to Vegas (I-15 Freeway) and entered into a no man's land, devoid of buildings or people.

As they approached what appeared to be abandoned railroad tracks, there was a wooden sign stating 'Afton Canyon Campground.' They turned off the road on to a graveled campground road, where they drove past a large sign listing the campground rules. As Shane continually turned his head from side to side to survey the campground, his car traveled straight forward. Eventually he found himself at the end of the campground road, staring at an empty campsite. By this time, he was convinced that the campground was totally empty of any cars, campers, or for that matter any living human beings.

Since they had the campground to themselves, the next order of business was where to start digging the grave. He wanted a remote site, but not too out of the way since Shane didn't want the cars to become stuck in the soft sand. After scouting around, they found what they thought was the best location behind the brush at the furthest campsite.

It was approaching 6:00 a. m. and the rays of the sun were flickering on the skyline. Both Shane and Frandsen were urban dwellers and they weren't seasoned shovel diggers. They took the shovel and poked it into the ground, trying to find some soft soil that would be easy to dig. They found a recessed area behind a row of brush. After they had cut through several pencil-sized roots from the brush, the shovel sliced through the sand with ease. It didn't take these city boys long before they realized it was wiser to throw the dug-out sand further from the hole.

In the last four hours, these young men had experienced so much that they were emotionally drained. An adrenaline high motivated their bodies to continue on and find a way to escape from being caught for murder. They were sweating profusely in the cool desert breeze as they continued to dig deeper and deeper. Neither was an expert grave digger, but the survival part of their brain told them the deeper the grave, the less likely it was that they would ever get caught. Out of fear, they had carved a gravesite which was six feet in length and three feet in width, and with a great deal of effort had reached a depth of four feet. As the minutes clicked by, the sun continued to rise higher and the rays of light ignited the horizon. As the sun rose, so did the intense desert heat. This was compounded by the two men's anxiety level. The daylight brought the fear that someone might pull into the campground and see them digging. What if they started asking questions?

Their plan was to remove all forms of identification from the victims. That included removing wallets, watches, jewelry, or anything found in the dead men's pockets. To further reduce the likelihood that anyone would be able to identify the bodies, their plan was to also remove all their clothing. They recognized that they were at the point of no return and needed to expeditiously bury the bodies. Shane directed Frandsen to back up the Chevy Cavalier as close to the grave as possible. When Frandsen was getting too close to the deep hole, Shane panicked that the car might fall in.

Shane yelled at Frandsen to stop, which he did. Although he could have backed up further, Shane didn't want to take chances. He directed Frandsen to push the trunk release button, which he did. The trunk popped open, revealing the victims. What the gravediggers weren't ready for was the stench from the dead bodies that permeated the fresh desert air.

Out of fear of being caught, the two men leaned into the trunk and grabbed whatever limbs they could reach. Grabbing legs and hands, they pulled the corpses out of the trunk.

Each body was pulled a short distance to the side of the deep hole, which would momentarily become a grave. At this point, they became aware it was going to take time to remove the clothing and shoes. How were they going to dispose of those removed items? Shane, at the last minute, decided to leave the clothes on the bodies after all forms of identification had been removed.

After pawing through the victims' pockets, it was time to pick up the bodies one by one and with a hard yank toss the men's bodies unceremoniously into the large grave. Adar's body was thrown in first and it settled to the bottom. Next Ben's body was flung into the grave, landing on top of his childhood friend. At that moment in time, Shane and Frandsen stared at each other with a feeling of accomplishment.

As soon as they filled the grave with soil, their problems would be buried deep beneath the earth. So Frandsen grabbed the shovel and frantically scooped the sand back into the grave. But Shane stood off to the side and seemed to hesitate. He glanced at Frandsen and thought, "Why don't I kill him, and then there will be no witnesses?" As Shane was contemplating how to kill his buddy, Frandsen, his eyes caught sight of the two cars. Then the realization hit him that he needed Frandsen to drive Ben's car to Vegas, where he would use it to create the illusion that Ben and Adar had arrived in there. Shane slowly moved over to Frandsen and told him to stomp on the sand to compress the soil. Shane took the shovel from him and started scooping the soil into the hole. Within minutes, the hole had been filled in.

Then they noticed they had additional sand left over, which most killers stack in a mound on top of the grave. Shane was smart enough to make sure they didn't leave any telltale signs, so he smoothed out the excess soil so anyone walking by would be unaware two young men's bodies lay buried four feet down under.

CHAPTER 13—ARRIVAL IN VEGAS

Shane had to be pleased how well the disposal of the bodies had gone. As they got back into the cars, Shane had a satisfying expression on his face. All the MBA courses he took at UCLA had been worth it. Even though there were no classes on killing people or burying bodies, he had learned how to stay focused in stressful situations. He never lost sight of his goal, which was to get away with murder.

They pulled their respective vehicles out of the campground and maneuvered the rocky road back to the freeway where they made a right turn, leading them to Vegas. Within 15 minutes, they saw a large freeway sign stating the turnoff to "ZZYZX Road." Everyone traveling to Las Vegas wonders if they need new glasses, or could a Cal Trans worker be playing a joke on them? In reality, this road leads to a community by the same name consisting of a population of two or three people, depending on the time of year.

In less than five minutes, the I-15 Freeway would bring them down the hill into the City of Baker, which is maybe considered an oasis to some who are hungry or in need of filling up their gas tanks. It is littered with service stations and fast food stands. Visitors who are approaching Baker are subjected to dozens of billboards advertising 'The Mad Greek' restaurant with all their Gyros and Shish Kebabs. At first it seems like a mirage. Who in their right mind wants Greek food out in the middle of the desert? Baker is the turnoff for those who have the urge or need to go to Death Valley, which is the lowest and hottest place in America. Without a doubt, the City of Baker is the center to nowhere. The main highlight for this city is that it has the tallest thermometer in the world, which all the motorists can read from the freeway as they zip by. Fortunately for Shane and Frandsen it registered a comfortable 48 Fahrenheit; however, in the summer it can spike its way up to125 degrees.

They could now sit back and put the cars in auto-drive, since the freeway straightens out in Baker, and they continued to cruise into Stateline. For any first timers to Vegas this can be mistaken for the gambling mecca in the desert. This area of casinos and hotels was built for the obsessed gamblers who can't wait another 45 minutes to start placing their bets in the real Vegas. Shane and Frandsen zoomed past Whiskey Pete's Hotel and Casino, which has displayed in its lobby Bonny and Clyde's 'Model A' Ford peppered with bullet holes. Maybe Shane didn't want to stop because he felt superior to those killers who got caught. His venturesome trip to Nevada and his idea of planting Ben's car could be described as brilliant and an ironclad guarantee he would never end up like Bonny and Clyde.

It wasn't long before they were rolling down the Vegas strip ignoring the historic past of where the old Hacienda Hotel was located for so many years, which was the beacon to announce one's arrival to Vegas. As they turned off the freeway, they zoomed past the Tropicana Casino Hotel, which headlined so many of the top stars of Vegas. They drove by the site of the old Dunes Hotel where Howard Hughes had lived when he dominated the Vegas landscape. Proceeding down the strip, they passed the Bellagio on the left, where visitors are bedazzled by the dancing water show.

Across from the Bellagio was a gigantic gaudy sign publicizing Bally's Jubilee Show, which had been showcasing for over a half a century by claiming to have the most beautiful showgirls in a topless extravaganza. Directly across the street was the old familiar Flamingo that was built in 1946 by Bugsy Siegel and his underworld crowd. Farther down the Strip, they drove by the site of the old Sands Hotel, where the "Rat Pack" hung out. The marquee no longer flashed the names from the mid 60s of Frank Sinatra, Dean Martin, Sammy Davis Jr., Peter Lawford, or Joey Bishop.

By noon, Shane and Frandsen had blended in with all the other thousands of tourists visiting Vegas. Upon their arrival, they weren't intoxicated by the lure to gamble or drink in the sports bars. All they wanted to do was get some sleep and clean up from their arduous grave digging. Their adrenaline high had faded into exhaustion. Shane found a hotel that met their basic needs and provided them some time to re-group their thoughts, as to the next phase of their coverup plot.

By late afternoon, they had recharged their human batteries and were ready for the next phase of their venture. High on that list was the placement of Ben's car so it would be discovered in Vegas. The police would presume the young men had traveled there on their own and somehow disappeared. Sometime after 4:32 p.m. on December 3rd, Frandsen drove Ben's car and parked it in front of a parking meter, on a street near an annex station for the Las Vegas Metropolitan Police Department. It wouldn't take long before the police would notice the abandoned car.

First they had to clean the car by wiping their fingerprints off everything they may have touched. In order to encourage passersby to take items, they rolled down the windows and left the keys in the unlocked car. On the front seat they placed

Ben's cellphone and some other identification. The only thing they didn't do was place a sign saying "Steal Me." After they had set everything up, Frandsen exited Ben's old Chevy and sat down in Shane's car and they quietly drove away hoping that someone would take the bait and steal the property, if not take the car.

It wasn't long before the parking meter ran out of time and the red "Expired" sign popped up in the parking meter's window. A 'meter maid' at 6:41 p.m. came by and noticed the meter had expired. She stopped and wrote a parking citation and placed it under the windshield wiper.

Shortly after Shane and Frandsen had taken care of the placement of the car, they started receiving phone calls from their friends in L.A. Now that it was December, it turned dark early, and it was only 20 days before the winter solstice—the shortest day of the year. Shane was called by his friend Khachatouian (the Russian Guy) wanting to know what had happened. Then around 6:00 p. m. Tuttle, Frandsen's roommate, called for an update as to what Shane and Frandsen were doing. Shane told Tuttle they were gambling in a casino. Tuttle could clearly hear in the background the slot machine's sounds of jangly music, the whir of the spinning reels accompanied by loud beeps and chimes.

Before they buried the bodies, Shane had attempted to take all the identification off the two victims. While doing so, he discovered credit cards in Adar Ne'eman's name. Shane comprehended an opportunity to leave a trail of credit card receipts throughout Vegas. This would further corroborate that Adar and Ben had arrived in Vegas, as could be seen from the purchases on the credit card. Shane didn't know what the maximum limit was on the credit cards, so in order to find out, they started using the cards to buy big-ticket items.

They attempted to purchase electronics equipment from a Best Buy store. It was 7:37 p.m. on December 3rd when they tried to purchase computer equipment that totaled $8,000. The cashier tried to run the American Express credit card through the system, but the transaction wouldn't go through. This may have been caused by the fact that Adar's credit card had a limit less than that amount.

They gave up on making big-ticket purchases and concentrated on regular retail outlets. They moved on to the "Catwalk" at 1040 E Flamingo Blvd., which was a trendy clothing and accessory store. Since they had spent several hours in the early hours digging a grave, their clothing had gotten dirty, so the idea was to replace their soiled clothes. Frandsen wanted to get some new pants, so he selected, a stylish velour, which was in his size. They purchased more clothes and Shane selected some Demonia Star shoes. These were unique elevator shoes with large colored stars around the outside. Even though Shane was 6 feet tall and didn't need elevator shoes, he felt the two inches made him taller and gave him a distinguished look.

After charging $467.87 worth of new clothes on Adar's Master Card, Shane and Frandsen were ready to show off their new acquisitions. They went to the 'Outback Steakhouse,' which features Australian cuisine. There they sat down to enjoy a scrumptious steak dinner with drinks and all the trimmings. Reviewing the prices wasn't necessary since it wasn't coming out of their pocket. When it was time to pay the bill, they charged it to Adar's credit card. The idea of using the victim's credit card proved to be doubly beneficial, in that they were able to make it appear as though the victims had been in Vegas, as well as ending up with some stylish clothes for themselves and a delicious dinner.

(The following graphic page shows the exhibits used to illustrate where Ben's car was parked in Las Vegas. The other exhibit shows that Adair's credit card was used to purchase Demonia shoes as well as the pants.)

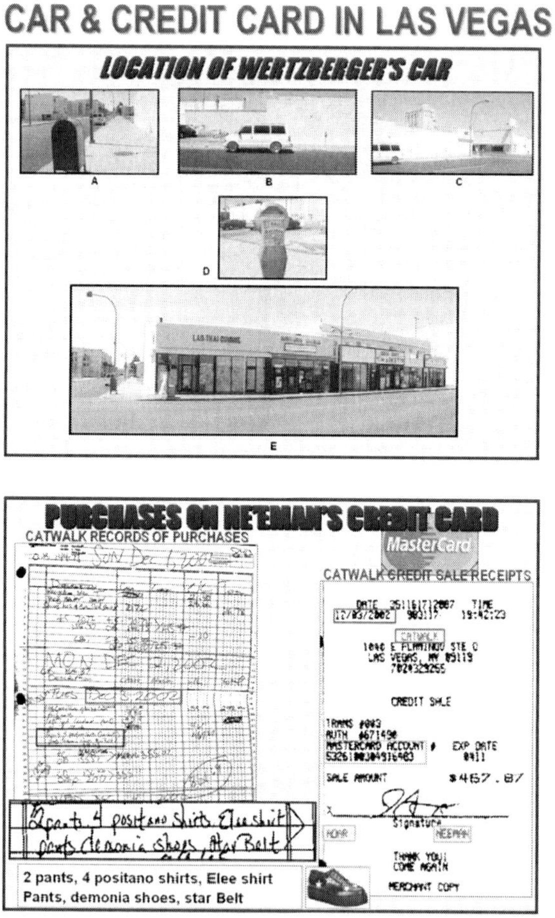

CHAPTER 14—LEAVING VEGAS, HEADING HOME

After a relaxing evening and a peaceful night's sleep, Shane and Frandsen prepared to depart Sin City and return to L.A. in Shane's Mustang. Traffic on a Wednesday morning for the drive back would be a breeze and they should make it home in five hours. They cruised the I-15 to the I-10, which brought them into the L.A. Civic Center several blocks from Chinatown. Shane drove Frandsen to the apartment that he shared with Tuttle. They went in and paraded around in their new fashionable clothing. Frandsen showed off his new velour pants and Shane strutted around in his new colorful Demonia Star shoes that made him feel ten feet tall. What made it even better was they didn't have to pay for anything, since they charged it all on Adar's credit card.

Directly upon Shane's return to L. A., he called his classmate, David Sherwood, who he was collaborating with in writing his Master's Degree project. He told Sherwood that he was back in town and ready to finish up the assignment. The two of them agreed to get together the following day.

Shane, having left Frandsen's apartment, went to visit Denton, his old friend from Venice. They discussed what had happened to the two guys who had ripped

Shane off. Shane replied, "We really fucked them up good." Shane didn't elaborate as to exactly what they had done to them and Denton was smart enough not to ask.

Life continued for Shane and Frandsen as though nothing had happened. Shane moved out of his place in Venice so he could live full-time in the little pink house on De Soto Avenue in Canoga Park. Since Shane was living on the premises, he could better oversee his property. For the next several months, there wasn't much activity going on since it was the holiday season and a time to be jolly and bright.

CHAPTER 15—THE FBI TO THE RESCUE

Time marched on. Since Shane became a full-time resident at the pink house he started putting his own personal touch in order to transform the place into a true bachelor pad. In late Spring he finished up his MBA at UCLA, graduating with honors. As a result of his academic accomplishments, his business career took off with him landing a prestigious position with one of the top financial firms in downtown. At the same time, Ben and Adar's mothers were trying to find out what had happened to their missing sons.

The most that was known was that Adar had arrived in Los Angeles on November 29, 2002, and four days later he disappeared. It was also known that Adar had been visiting with his friend Ben Wertzberger in the Los Angeles area. After several expensive but futile attempts using private investigators, the mothers had pressured authorities to conduct an investigation into the disappearance of their sons. The finding of Ben's car and the use of Adar's credit card in Vegas made it appear as if both young men had crossed the state line, which provided a rationale for the FBI getting involved in the investigation.

Agent Mark Williams had more than enough "Open" investigations that he was supervising. The FBI didn't need to take on any additional cases. But the agent could feel the anguish the mothers were going through. He agreed the FBI would do a cursory investigation and see where it would lead. He assigned the task to two very energetic FBI agents, David Clouse and Kelly Dempsey. The mothers were instructed to meet with those two agents and provide them with all the information that the mothers had uncovered through their private investigators.

Initially there didn't seem to be anything tangible that could be done to find the two missing young men. This wasn't an orthodox type investigation that FBI agents usually become involved in. Where do you start and what needs to be done? One approach was to try to prove the young men had voluntarily disappeared in order to have some fun. Another theory was that the men were trying to escape the grasp of a loan shark they owed money to. Or, on a more ominous note, the men had met with foul play somewhere in this country.

The agents reviewed what the PI had done and studied the leads from the use of the credit card and the impounding of Ben's car in Vegas. The agents wanted to pursue the fact that Ben Wertzberger's cellphone had been traced and had been used in December by a hooker in the Vegas area. When the agents received the cellphone information, they noticed that in the month of November there had been numerous calls to a cellphone number that was registered to a Shane Huang.

From that point on, the agents could see that Ben and Shane had been in constant contact for over a month. The agents went one step further and obtained a search warrant for Shane's cellphone records. The result showed numerous phone calls to Ben Frandsen, Jamil Khachatouian, Nick Tuttle, and Joe Pierson. Then the agents obtained search warrants of all of the parties' phone records. What was soon revealed was a pattern of phone calls made by Shane to all these other people.

The best the agents came up with was a friend of Ben Wertzberger who claimed Ben was on his way to the San Fernando Valley to pay back someone who had loaned him money. That person said that he didn't know what was going on but that the agents should contact a Joe Pierson, aka 'The Plumber Man.' Since the agents weren't coming up with much else, they followed through and located Pierson, who met with them. Pierson didn't know why the FBI was asking him all these questions. Pierson, for whatever reason, started telling the agents a very strange story. He said that Shane had called him on December 2nd and said that he had caught a kid by the name of Berger, which in fact was Wertzberger, climbing into a back window of his place on De Soto Avenue in the San Fernando Valley. Shane took the matter into his own hands and held Berger and his companion by the use of a large sword. Pierson described how Shane and Frandsen held these guys until he left later in the evening. Pierson indicated that Nick Tuttle could provide them with even more information. No one claimed to know anything about the disappearance of the two young men. Everyone agreed that the missing men were in the company of Shane and Frandsen during the early morning hours of December 3rd.

By April 8, 2003, the agents obtained a search warrant for the pink house on De Soto Avenue where Shane was living. Upon their search of the location, the agents found a sword and some type of martial arts equipment. Since the search warrant was directed for the seizure of drugs, the agents couldn't seize the sword, but they made a note of its existence.

CHAPTER 16—LOOKING FOR EVIDENCE

By spring of 2002, the investigation hadn't uncovered any 'smoking gun' type of evidence or anything useful. At this point no murder weapon had been found, no bodies had been discovered, and no one even knew if anyone had been killed. The most the agents had learned was that Ben had previously lived in the pink house. Also, several people had indicated that they had last seen Ben and another guy at the De Soto house.

The agents wanted to obtain everyone's statements separately. This technique paid off. They interviewed Jamil Khachatouian, who didn't want to say much about the two young men detained at Shane's place. As the agents pressed Shane's friends for details, none of them wanted to commit to any one story of the events. The agents hoped they could crack into the conscience of one of them to open up and reveal the true facts.

Yet, nothing worked according to plan. The agents were informed that Jamil had left the country for his native Czech Republic with intentions never to return. Shane's confederates could feel the heat and started to break ranks. If they didn't start telling the truth, they might find themselves being charged with 'False Imprisonment' for their role in holding the two men against their will.

By September of 2003, the agents had started to build a case against Shane and Frandsen. Both Tuttle and Pierson supplied incriminating information that Shane had threatened the two victims. Everyone wanted to make it appear that they didn't do anything wrong. Their spin of the facts took on the scenario they helped protect the victims from the abuse initiated by Shane.

On September 14th, the FBI obtained another search warrant and conducted a third search of the De Soto address. This time the warrant included a search for weapons and money. The agents took the sword and nunchucks as well as an old sawed-off rifle. Shane, at the same time, was arrested by the agents. They advised him of his Miranda Rights, which he waived, agreeing to talk to the agents.

Shane had gone 10 months without being arrested, and this length of time only reassured him that he could outsmart any 'gum-chewing detective.' He projected an egotistical air of invincibility that he could confidently handle any amount of questioning. He had no fear of talking to the two FBI agents. Self-absorbed and arrogant might be words to best describe his attitude. When the agents started their inquiry as to what Shane knew about the missing men, Shane admitted that he and Ben Wertzberger had a little dispute over money owed to Shane. He said, however, that it was all resolved when Ben agreed to pay him back for what had been owed. After they came to terms, the young men left and went their separate ways. He further stated that he didn't travel to Las Vegas or have anything to do with using Adar's credit cards in Vegas. The interrogation concluded and the agents hadn't obtained anything useful.

Frandsen had moved away from the L.A. scene and taken a job working at Yellowstone National Park. Agents Kelly Dempsey and David Clouse traveled to Yellowstone to interview him at the Old Faithful ranger station. There they advised Frandsen of his Miranda Rights and asked him if he would waive his rights and talk to them without an attorney. Frandsen couldn't be considered on the same intellectual level as Shane. He would best be described as Shane's unsophisticated puppet. When the agents asked detailed questions, Frandsen didn't know how to answer and undoubtedly wished he could consult with Shane before responding.

As the interrogation proceeded, Frandsen began to slowly disclose certain facts as to what happened that fateful day of the murders. He wanted to minimize his involvement but spelled out how Shane became enraged with Ben. Shane had convinced himself that Ben had stolen his marijuana and money. Eventually, Frandsen admitted to helping Shane in restraining the two young men while they figured out what to do with them. Frandsen was amenable to explaining the events on the evening where they held the two young men. Conversely, he danced around the question of his involvement in the killing of the two.

He gave several versions as to how the killings occurred. He said Shane actually took Ben into the bathroom, where he tried to drown him. Frandsen's version stated that Shane strangled Ben. Originally, he claimed the killing of Adar could be considered an accident, then later it became self-defense, and ultimately, Adar ran into Shane's extended arm, which broke Adar's neck. Whatever version one took, Frandsen had admitted to being present with Shane at the time the two young men were killed.

Up to this point, the FBI agents had little evidence on Shane, unless they wanted to give immunity to Frandsen and have him testify against Shane. That prospect didn't look good, since they wanted to be able to make murder cases against both Shane and Frandsen.

CHAPTER 17—IMPORTANCE IN FINDING BODIES

At that point in time, the agents had a significant legal issue with their case. They had not found the bodies of the victims. That can be a major impediment in any homicide case. American criminal law has its genesis in English Common Law. There have been several areas where English Common Law has created insurmountable obstacles, preventing prosecutors from charging and convicting murderers when the victim's body has not been recovered.

The reason for these restrictions occurred hundreds of years ago in England when several defendants were convicted of murder, even though the bodies of the victims had not been found. The defendants were suspected of the killings because they had the most to benefit from the death of the victims. These defendants were convicted in the court and punished by execution. However, several years later the victims reappeared, and at that point it was too late to bring the executed defendants back to life.

To minimize this type of catastrophe, English law established a rule that a murder conviction couldn't stand unless there was direct evidence on one of the two elements of the 'corpus delicti,' which consisted in the death of the victim and the criminal means by which it was caused. This resulted in the "corpus delicti" law, meaning the prosecution has to prove that a crime has been committed before the defendant's confession can be introduced as evidence. In other words, the crime can't be proven by the defendant's admission that he committed a crime.

Some people interpreted the "corpus delicti" law to mean that the prosecution must produce evidence that the victim was in fact dead. The courts wanted testimony of a coroner or medical examiner to review the remains of a corpse and establish that in fact the victim had indeed been killed. The unintended result was that if a killer was good at disposing of the victim's body so it was never found then the body could not be examined by a coroner, and therefore the killer could not be convicted of murder. The appellate court quickly realized that such a strict 'corpus delicti' rule would allow murderers to get away with murder.

At this point, the courts carved out the exception that if "criminal means or agency" were present then that could prove the so-called 'corpus delicti' requirement. This could be done by using direct evidence, such as an eyewitness who saw the victim being killed, even though later there was no body found by authorities.

The biggest break for prosecutors occurred when the appellate courts agreed that circumstantial evidence could be used to prove the 'corpus delicti.' Evidence of a crime scene such as blood or presence of weapons could supply the 'corpus delicti' requirement.

In this case, during the original investigation Ben's and Adar's bodies had not been found, meaning that the 'corpus delicti' law would apply. Was there any circumstantial evidence to prove the 'corpus delicti'? In this case, no murder weapon was ever found. Also, there was no evidence of a crime scene where there was blood or any signs of a struggle. In this case, Shane had made sure to clean up the pink house so nothing could be found later. The agents realized the importance of finding the bodies if they ever hoped to prosecute Shane for murder.

The agents knew that Shane would never reveal the gravesite. Would Frandsen be willing to disclose the burial site? The agents started a lengthy and tedious questioning of Frandsen. For some unexplainable reason, Frandsen didn't want to admit to the burial of the victims. He continued to be vague as to the victims' gravesite. The agents got him to concede that the victims were buried on the road to Vegas. The agents knew there was no way they could find the bodies with such a vague description. After eight hours, the interrogation of Frandsen had to be concluded. The hopes of the Israeli mothers and concerns of thousands of Israelis who had followed the plight of this case on national TV would be dashed. Without more detailed information about the burial site, the successful prosecution of both killers was unlikely.

Since Frandsen had been arrested, Special Agents David Clouse and Kelly Dempsey were waiting for someone to take Frandsen to a jail facility. The interview had been finished and the tape recorders had been put away. Everyone felt exhausted, especially Frandsen, who had tried to talk his way out of being arrested for murder. Both agents had had a particularly long day, since they had flown to Yellowstone and driven to the ranger station where Frandsen worked as an employee. Both agents were extremely professional and certainly would be considered unobtrusive compared too many of the old-time homicide detectives from LAPD or LASD.

Throughout the interrogation with Frandsen, they were persistent but polite. When it was over, they continued to try and determine what could be done with his personal items. Since he was being arrested, who should receive his property? They were trying to work with Frandsen as to where to send his private stuff.

Just before being taken away by the jailer, Frandsen leaned over to the agents and in a consoling voice said, "I know there was like a blue metallic building off the freeway. There was a sign on the building that said something about an internet site. The sign said something like, www.net or.com." Then he added, "There was a campground at the end of a dirt road."

Frandsen was escorted away by the jailer as the two agents stood at the doorway. Both looked at each other in disbelief. The comment was made, "Where was a tape recorder when you needed it?" One of the agents sat down and scrawled on a piece of paper what Frandsen had just related to them. The agents realized that someday in court they would be cross-examined as to why this wasn't part of a tape-recorded statement. Some defense attorneys would try to infer the agents had made this up. The agents didn't care that they might be criticized for not recording this statement.

The fact that there wasn't a tape recorder may have been the reason Frandsen felt comfortable in making this revelation. The agents realized the words he had spoken had given them the best chance to find the bodies, which would allow them to construct a credible case against both Shane and Frandsen.

CHAPTER 18—EUREKA WE FOUND THEM!

With Frandsen providing the key to solving the mystery, it was a matter of time and a stroke of luck that the victims' bodies were found, not to mention a curious cadaver dog. As we have previously discussed, the actual discovery occurred when the agents and staff were digging the soft sand, shovel by shovel, and a shoe was spotted. When it was realized that the shoe was attached to a body, the 'Eureka' moment occurred. At the moment, they knew it time to go into the 'protect the evidence' mode. There is one procedure for searching; however, there is an entirely different protocol when a location becomes a crime scene.

The FBI agents called in the San Bernardino County Sheriff & Coroner's Office to remove the bodies from the hole. Fortunately, in that county the Sheriff and Coroner are combined into one agency. The benefit was that there wouldn't be two separate entities having to respond, since they are all in one. The area had been elevated to an active crime scene. The gravesite region was laid out in a nine-foot-by-nine-foot grid along magnetic north and south. All depth and position references were made using this grid. Anything found within the area would receive a grid number. This made it easier to explain the relationship between various items that were uncovered.

At 8:28 a.m., the Coroner's Office was notified, and shortly thereafter an investigator from their headquarters, in downtown San Bernardino, was dispatched. In the meantime, the FBI, with their own Forensic Anthropologist, continued to examine the gravesite. After using paint brushes to sweep away the loose dirt, they proceeded to use spoon-like scoopers to dig out the soil and placed it in small buckets. Ultimately, the dirt was then sifted through a 1/8th inch screen. As tedious as this process seemed, it was necessary to find and preserve any other evidence around or near the body.

The agents had to make some decisions as to how to proceed without a perfect environment. It was mid-September, when temperatures in the area can easily soar to over 115 degrees Fahrenheit, and in the afternoon the intensity of the wind can be blinding. Erecting an 'EZ Up' sun tarp over the grave made the process a little more tolerable by blocking the intense sun, but it had to be well secured to prevent it from sailing airborne. It was imperative that they swiftly proceed with what they could do, since it would be four hours before the coroner's investigator would arrive on the scene. They continued to remove the dirt from the gravesite so they could determine if there were two bodies in this one grave, or whether they needed to continue to search for another gravesite.

By noon, the FBI concluded that another body was under the top one. Great news, since there was no need to continue the search for another grave. At 12:21p.m., the coroner's investigator arrived and took charge of removing the bodies from the hole. He wrote in his report, "The bodies were in an advanced state of decomposition, with desiccation of portions of the skin, but liquefaction of much of the soft tissue." He further noted that both bodies were clad in a t-shirt, jeans, and white socks.

In order not to mix up the two bodies, he described what he did to both bodies, "A toe tag number was affixed to their right foot. The bodies were removed from the grave and placed into separate yellow plastic body pouches, which were in turn placed into a separate black heavy-duty fabric body pouch with handles."

The top corpse was that of Ben Wertzberger, and he still had on one of his fingers a scorpion ring, which he always wore. He was removed first, and then Adar Ne'eman's body was found underneath. Due to the extent of the deterioration of the bodies, it couldn't be determined how the two victims were killed. The investigator used a metal detector to pass over the bottom of the gravesite and over all the soil that had been removed to see if any bullet fragments could be found.

The depth of the grave was measured and found to be 49 inches. Once the bodies were removed, the grave was filled in and the two body bags were placed in the coroner's van at 5:28 p. m. and it headed to the Central Coroner's Morgue Facility in downtown San Bernardino, where the two body bags were placed in the refrigeration unit.

CHAPTER 19—WHAT'S THE CAUSE OF DEATH?

On September 24, the agents met at the morgue for the autopsy, which was to be performed by Dr. Steven Trenkle, a Forensic Pathologist. He had gained his training and experience from a long line of medical schools starting with USC and Loma Linda, as well as UC San Francisco. He had performed over 2500 autopsies, mainly for San Bernardino County. This county is the largest geographical county in the USA and is made up of hundreds of square miles of desert stretching from the Los Angeles County border all the way to the Colorado River, which borders the state of Arizona. What this meant was that Dr. Trenkle had seen more than his share of decomposed bodies that had been dumped in the desert.

He was the perfect coroner to examine the decomposed bodies of Ben and Adar. Often coroners and pathologists will not render an opinion on decomposed bodies, because bullet holes and stab wounds can't be observed since the soft tissue areas have decomposed.

Ben's autopsy was conducted first. The coroner examined the remains for any signs of injury, such as a knife or bullet wound or a blunt force trauma injury. Because of the severe decomposition, he was not able to note any injuries, but he was still able to determine the cause of death to be "Homicidal Violence." He came to that opinion based on the fact that there were two bodies found buried together in the desert.

When he had finished with Ben's autopsy everything was put away, so he could get started on Adar's autopsy. The coroner's staff had removed Adar's body bag from the refrigeration unit. The bag had been unzipped and the yellow plastic bag was opened up on a gurney. X-rays had been taken of the remains to determine if there might be any bullets obscured somewhere in the body. Nothing was found, and the body was made ready for the autopsy by removing dirt and debris. Dr. Trenkle started his cursory observation of the body, and as he got to the neck region he became fixated on the neck bones and the cartilage that formed the voice box or larynx. He could make out that the thyroid cartilage in the front of the neck, better described as the "Adam's Apple" had been fractured on the left side. He pointed this out to the agents watching the autopsy, stating, "There's your blunt force trauma." He went on to explain that could be the fatal injury.

Next he concentrated on the back of the neck, in particular the cervical vertebra, and noticed that it had been split or fractured. One of the agents asked, "What's your opinion as to the cause of death of Adar Ne'eman?" He indicated that it was 'Blunt Force Neck Injuries.' He went on to say that the manner of death was definitively "Homicide."

He explained his reasoning as follows: "In this case, it was the circumstances of the disappearance of the two men, and then, the way they were found, buried out in the desert that led to the 'homicidal' designation for the manner of death."

Because of the type of neck injuries, Dr. Trenkle indicated that he had to remove the neck bones from the rest of the corpse and have them put through scientific tests to confirm his findings. Unfortunately, the dental expert would not be able to compare the dental records until Friday. Agent Kelly Dempsey had brought out the dental records she had received from the Israeli military for both Ben and Adar. They were given to the coroner's office to be forwarded to Dr. Golden, a Forensic Odontologist, who later did an examination of the remains and compared them to the Israeli military dental X-rays. His finding was that Victim #1, who was found on the top in the grave, was definitely Ben Wertzberger, and likewise Victim #2, was Adar Ne'eman.

Those findings were given to Agent Kelly Dempsey, who had the task of notifying the parents of this unfortunate information, although it wasn't unexpected. The parents were notified, and they asked to have the remains of both their sons released so they could be flown back to Israel for a proper Jewish burial. The coroner's office indicated that they couldn't release the bodies until the U.S. Attorney's Office agreed they would not be needed for any further evidentiary purposes.

Rabbis from Los Angeles, and even New York, became involved on behalf of the victims' families. The Jewish custom required the deceased must be immediately buried. The State Department became embroiled, and pressure was placed on the U.S. Attorney to quickly release the bodies. After numerous phone calls between the parties, a tentative agreement was reached that the bodies would be released as long as the coroner retained the neck bones showing the fracture. This could be made available to the defense attorneys, who could have it examined by their own expert pathologist.

It seemed like an international dispute had been resolved. However, the rabbis objected since Jewish culture required that all parts of the body must be buried at the same time. In other words, Adar's remains couldn't be buried without the neck bones, which showed the blunt force trauma. This caused a great deal of concern to law enforcement authorities, and the coroner's office wondered if, in the interest of cultural sensitivity, something could be worked out by taking numerous photos or videos of the neck bones.

After considerable time went by, it seemed a solution could be worked out with the U.S. Attorney's Office. Then it was announced that the prosecution of the criminal case might be turned over to the Los Angeles District Attorney's Office. The DA knew nothing about this case, so the DA took the position not to release the remains until they had made a determination as to the value of the neck bones for trial. Bottom line was, as if Adar Ne'eman parents hadn't suffered enough, they were going to have wait even longer before they would be able to properly bury their son.

CHAPTER 20—WHO IS GOING TO PROSECUTE THIS CASE?

For the FBI to become involved in a criminal matter, it is generally required that it be some type of federal crime. When the FBI is working on a criminal matter, they naturally take it to the U.S. Attorney's Office, which handles the prosecution of federal offenses. This case was no different, so the FBI agents took the case to the U.S. Attorney's Office in Los Angeles so it could be presented to a federal grand jury. On September 26, 2003, a grand jury indicted both Shane and Frandsen for the crime of kidnapping, resulting in the death of the victims. When Nick Tuttle, the roommate of Frandsen, was arrested, the matter was resubmitted to the grand jury and Tuttle was indicted for aiding and abetting in the kidnapping.

The most common types of federal offenses are bank robbery, counterfeiting, drug smuggling, and kidnapping across state lines. However, when the agents obtained statements from Frandsen, he claimed that the victims were kidnapped and killed in the Canoga Park house and the victims had never been taken across state lines either dead or alive.

Yet, there is another federal kidnapping crime which doesn't involve going across state lines. This is the one used against Shane and Frandsen which is worded as follows: "Whoever unlawfully seizes, confines, inveigles, decoys, **kidnaps**, abducts, or carries away and holds for ransom or reward or otherwise any person when any such act against the person **done within the special maritime and territorial jurisdiction** of the United States. (18U.S. C. sec. 1201(a)(2))." This would seem to fit the situation in this case, since the bodies were buried within the Afton Canyon Campground, which is on Federal Bureau of Land Management property.

As time went by, one of the U.S. attorneys looked into the matter and found that they didn't have jurisdiction to prosecute this case. In order for the matter to be brought into the federal courts, they had to prove that Afton Canyon Campground was within the words in the statute 'special maritime and territorial jurisdiction.' In order to qualify, the U.S. must have acquired this land for a 'fort, magazine arsenal, dockyard, or other needful buildings.'

Anyone entering this desolate land of the Afton Canyon Campground would never think of this Bureau of Land Management site as a **fort, arsenal, or dockyard**. Therefore, the federal kidnapping statute didn't apply. With that information, the U.S. Attorney's Office most likely couldn't contain their enthusiasm by yelling, "Thank God we got rid of that case." It will never be known what the real motivation was for the U.S. Attorney's Office in handing off this 'hot potato' of a case. Could it be they grasped how difficult it would be to prosecute Shane Huang? Or was it a real issue of not having jurisdiction?

What transpired next was that the U.S. Attorney's Office called up the District Attorney's Office and said, "Do we have a case for you!" The DA's Office felt they were about to be the recipient of a colossal can of worms delivered to their doorstep.

When the facts of the case were explained to the DA's Complaints Division, it was recognized that this case was going to need a lot of special attention. At that juncture, the DA's Major Crimes Division was asked to meet with the FBI agents to decide if the state court would have jurisdiction to handle this case.

Deputy DA Alan Jackson was told to review the case and see what it was all about. Alan realized that the state kidnapping statute would apply, therefore the FBI was advised to roll all the case boxes across the street to the DA's Office in the state's Criminal Courts Building.

Looking at this case, at first glance one could see that it would be an easy case against Frandsen, since he admitted to his involvement, especially in the killing of Adar. Conversely, as to Shane, no direct evidence connected him to the killings, with the exception of Frandsen's statements explaining Shane's involvement. Nevertheless, those statements couldn't be used against Shane unless the prosecution was to give Frandsen immunity. This case had a basic dilemma: either give Frandsen a free pass to get him to testify against Shane, or proceed with only Frandsen. To try and prosecute both Shane and Frandsen for murder, without some type of granting immunity, was a major problem.

Within short order all the boxes were in the DA's Office, and on June 22, 2004, a criminal complaint for two counts of murder were filed against Shane and Frandsen, accompanied by an aiding and abetting murder charge filed against Nick Tuttle.

CHAPTER 21—MOTION FOR SPEEDY TRIAL

All three defendants had separate attorneys. Shane wanted to be represented by the very best attorney that money could buy. He selected one of the most prominent attorneys in the entire county, Anthony Brooklier, who always made a formidable appearance in court with his tailored suits and bushy gray hair. He had been involved in many highly publicized cases, one in which he represented the Hollywood Madame, Heidi Fleiss. That type of case put him in the media spotlight. Brooklier had an impeccable reputation for being a strong litigator, knowing the law, and always projecting a confident demeanor in front of a jury.

Frandsen didn't have the funds to hire a private attorney; therefore, he received the services of an attorney from the Public Defender's Office. His attorney was experienced and knew his craft but was not in the same league as Shane's private attorney, Brooklier. Tuttle also had an appointed attorney, whose main goal was to negotiate some type of deal so Tuttle could plead to a lesser offense, such as accomplice or accessory. The prosecution wanted to reduce the number of defendants in this case, so everyone was motivated to work out a plea bargain. In just a matter, of time, Tuttle would be playing a legal form of 'musical chairs,' since he would move from one of the defendants' chairs to the prosecution witness's chair.

Due to the special nature and complexity of this case, the DA administrators assigned it to the Major Crimes Division. Deputy DA Shelly Samuels, who handled the major cases for the San Fernando Valley, became the lucky recipient of the case. A year earlier, she had been given the Robert Blake murder case for trial, especially since it had occurred in the San Fernando Valley, in particular just outside of Vitello's Restaurant in Studio City. Until the preliminary hearing commenced, Blake had been in custody and the case was moving swiftly through the system. At the end of the hearing, his attorney made an earnest request to the court to reduce Blake's bail. For whatever reason the judge reduced the bail and immediately, Blake bonded out and was back on the streets.

As a result, the Blake case went into slow motion, since nothing was motivating him to go to trial. Some court watchers believed the chance of a trial was nil and betting money was that Blake would die of natural causes before a jury ever saw or heard the first witness in his case. After numerous defense continuances, the judge recognized that the case was headed down the slippery slope of 'Justice Denied.' The judge put the defense on notice that there would be no further delays in the Blake case and a mandatory trial date was set. That meant prosecutor Shelly Samuels would be shortly starting the Blake trial and all her other cases would have to trail after the conclusion of the Blake case.

Major Crimes prosecutors carry a case load of five to six murder cases at any one time. The cases move through the system very slowly, and seldom do they go to trial at the same time. Often, the prosecutor has to reschedule his or her trial calendar and take into consideration other continuances. With the Blake case taking priority,

Samuels went into court on Shane and Frandsen's case and asked for a continuance until after the conclusion of the Blake case. All defendants have a right to a speedy trial and can demand to be tried within 60 days of the arraignment after their preliminary hearing. Seldom does a defense attorney object to such rescheduling. This is because defense attorneys know that they will have their own scheduling problems, and will undoubtedly have to ask for their own continuances in the future. To assure the prosecutor's cooperation, they will respectfully go along with a prosecutor's request for a continuance and talk their client into waiving their right to a speedy trial.

On the next court date, Deputy DA Samuels asked for a continuance, which was thought to be a mere formality. Frandsen's attorneys had no problem with the continuance request and agreed to a new date. However, Shane's attorney stated that his client would not agree to such a continuance and demanded a speedy trial. The prosecutor, Samuels, was shocked when Shane's defense attorney would not allow the case to go over so she could try the case.

Suddenly the DA's Office had a major predicament with Shane not going along with the continuance. This was a brilliant move on Shane's attorney's part. It had taken prosecutor Samuels considerable time to become familiar with the facts of Shane's case, as well as develop a rapport with the many witnesses, especially the victims' mothers. It would be extremely problematic for the DA's Office to bring in a new prosecutor to take over such a complex case. There were dozens of boxes of reports and multiple transcripts of witnesses' testimony that would have to be reviewed by a newly assigned prosecutor.

The DA's Office didn't want to go back into court on the Blake case and ask for that case to be continued. It had been the DA's Office who demanded the Blake case start trial, and they didn't want the judge to withdraw the mandatory trial date. The only option was for the DA's Office to reassign Shane's case to a new prosecutor so Deputy DA Samuels could start the Blake jury trial.

The DA's Office knew how unpopular this decision would be. Any prosecutor who was assigned Shane's case at such a late date would be furious that a double murder case had been dumped on him or her. Also, with this short notice there wasn't enough time in the remaining business days to read all the material. What it meant was that the new prosecutor would be required to give up his or her personal life for the next few months to read all the transcripts and FBI reports in order to be ready for trial.

The Robert Blake case was also being handled by the DA's Major Crimes Division since it was a high publicity case. Based on the fact that it was the Blake case that had created the dilemma, the DA's Office turned to the Major Crimes Division to assign one of their trial deputies to take over Shane's case. That Division was made up of the best of the best prosecutors that can be found in any DA's office. These prosecutors take pride in the meticulous way they organize their cases, making sure that every detail has been taken care of. Months and months of painstaking preparation goes into every one of their cases.

The supervisor of the Major Crimes Division had the daunting task of selecting the unlucky prosecutor who would be burdened with Shane's case. He realized that most of his attorneys were set for lengthy trials within the month. He reviewed the caseload of the other high-powered litigators in his Division. He knew they would go ballistic if such a big case were assigned to them. Who could he find to drop this bombshell on without it exploding into a meltdown of the Major Crimes Division?

CHAPTER 22—KARLA OF MAJOR CRIMES

Deputy District Attorney Karla Kerlin hurriedly raced into her windowed office on the 17th floor of the Criminal Courts Building. Her office had a breathtaking view of the mountains that surround Los Angeles. Some days she can only see out her windows a haze which was once called smog, but on this day the wind had cleared out the basin and the view of the San Gabriel Mountains was crystal clear.

Prosecutor Karla Kerlin would be described as tall in stature and strikingly attractive and would be classified as a 'head turner.' Anyone who meets her is captivated by her large bright eyes and the disarming smile that lights up her face. She is always appropriately dressed in with a well-tailored suit, which gives her the appearance of a professional woman who is on the move. Because of her previous career, she projects a cover-girl image, which gives others the idea of aloofness when in fact she can be very disarming with her down to earth comments. Once people get to know her, they recognize her outgoing, upbeat personality, which puts everyone at ease.

Her phone rang with the sound of urgency. Her hand lunged to the phone in hopes of catching it before it went to her voice mail. She was relieved when she heard a voice and not a dial tone. She paused for a moment to clear her voice and proceeded with the official office salutation, "This is Karla Kerlin, Deputy District Attorney of the Major Crimes Division, and how may I help you?" She was expecting a phone call from a news media inquiring about her recent murder trial, in which the jury swiftly returned with a First Degree Murder verdict. She seemed surprised when a woman's voice on the other end of the line asked, "Is this the Karla Kerlin, the Sexual Assault expert?"

Karla smirked to herself, thinking this must be a prank, or someone setting her up for some free advice on one of their Sexual Assault cases. Her suspicions were confirmed when the woman announced that she was in charge of arranging a mega conference on the East Coast that was addressing "Crimes Against Women." In a sleek, almost rehearsed spiel, the woman explained she had heard that Karla had been the top-rated speaker at several conferences the year before. Karla quickly realized where the conversation was going. Glancing over at her calendar, she could see that she was saturated with speaking engagements until the spring. With that information, she could gracefully refuse another speaking engagement by claiming that she was completely booked up.

Karla had mastered the Sexual Crime laws and over the years honed her skills to take on the unique challenges of prosecuting rapists and sexual predators. She knew how to build confidence with reluctant victims who were petrified to testify in a courtroom while their assaulter sat only a few feet away. The complexity of the scientific tests in rape cases can be daunting. Karla recognized the need to simplify the forensic evidence so jurors could comprehend what it all meant. She had conducted a myriad of training sessions for investigators and social workers to assist and to better prepare their Sexual Assault cases for court. Her fervent belief was that if investigators knew what was needed for court, the cases would be stronger with more evidence, resulting in more sexual predators being convicted and removed from the streets.

As the woman on the phone pitched the impact of her conference, Karla started a tug-a-war in her mind. Should she commit herself to another speaking engagement? Her husband had been more than understanding in the past, but she didn't want to push aside her duties as a wife. Her daughter was the center of their personal life, and she needed and wanted to spend more time with her. The speaking engagements were important, but so was her family.

Her last murder case had taken up so much of her time, since it had entailed a lengthy trial. The stresses and incredible demands on prosecutors during trial aren't compensated by the modest government salary they receive. However, the reward comes in other forms, such as the exhilarating moment when the smirky smile of a sexual predator is wiped off their face by the words of the courtroom clerk announcing the jury's verdict of 'GUILTY.' The tears of relief on a young victim's face when the rapist is convicted are the intangible benefits that Karla savored.

When the woman said the conference was in late spring, Karla without hesitation said, "Count me in." The woman seemed relieved and somewhat surprised at Karla's swift acceptance to the speaking engagement and told her she would e-mail her all the details. As Karla hung up the phone she noticed a folder piled on top of several open law books. The folder jogged her memory that she needed to make calls to line up a speaker for the next meeting of the Women Lawyers Association, of which she was president. That organization was another cause near and dear to her. One of the goals of the association was to encourage young women to enter the field of law. Karla felt women attorneys had mutual interests that often went unnoticed by the local bar associations and the courts. Her energy and active participation in the Women Lawyers Association had forced law firms and government agencies to pay more attention to women's needs.

CHAPTER 23—HAND OFF TO KARLA

Karla sat behind her timeworn county desk surveying her cluttered office with a wall of cardboard boxes filled with case files and documents from her latest murder trial. Outside her door were dozens of boxes lining the hallway. Only weeks before, the Fire Marshal had come by and threatened to write a citation for her maintaining an unsafe working environment. Only by the fast talking of the head secretary in the Major Crimes Division was a citation averted, on the condition that within the month all of Karla's boxes would be out of the hall. The irony of this situation was that a prosecutor, trying to convict the worst of the worst, was herself, in violation of the safety code by putting boxes in the hallways. The DA's Office had run out of space to store the boxes at their warehouse in the City of Commerce. Therefore, the attorneys had to be creative in finding space to store their boxes of old files.

In order not to get a criminal record, Karla wanted to keep her promise to the Fire Marshal. She felt obligated to box the finished murder case files and then move the boxes from the hall into her office. Since she had to appear in court that morning, Karla was dressed in a fashionable business suit and was reluctant to move all the dirty boxes that day. She decided to wait until Friday to do the heavy lifting, since the 'Friday dress code' permitted her to wear jeans, which would be more fitting for cleaning up her office.

Her office was becoming quite congested, but she could squeeze a few more boxes against the window. Out of the corner of her eye, she noticed the head deputy of Major Crimes had quietly walked into her office. She was pleased to see her boss since he always came by to congratulate his trial lawyers when they had won a tough case. The Major Crimes tradition was that the boss gave, from his private stock, a bottle of top-of-the-line champagne. Even though Karla didn't care much for the bubbly stuff, she did relish hearing the words "Job well done." Karla was like all other attorneys, who by their very nature like to be recognized and congratulated for their efforts. However, in this instance the boss's conversation didn't proceed as she had expected. His first words were an inquiry about her trial calendar and when her next trial would commence.

Karla grasped that this wasn't the typical "that-a-boy" chat. She was uncertain where this discussion was going. She responded that she had several pretrial motions and a couple of preliminary hearings, but the next trial was over a month away. Her boss seemed relieved on hearing this and without any fanfare stated, "I have a murder case that you are slightly familiar with because you helped out on the prelim." Karla turned her head to think of what prelim she had done for one of her fellow attorneys. The only case that came to mind was the one she helped Shelly Samuels out with when Shelly had an appearance on the Blake case. But Karla knew that couldn't be the case since it was supposed to trail until after the Blake case.

Her boss explained that the defense attorney, Brooklier, had refused to waive time on Shane's case, although the other attorney for Frandsen had agreed to the continuance. Shelly had to start the Blake case so the Shane case had to be 'handed off.' The picture was starting to be framed for Karla that she was inheriting the Shane Huang case. Things started flashing through Karla's mind. She remembered all the problems with the case and that none of the trial preparation had been done.

Karla knew about the real world. For years, the "old boy" network ruled and women attorneys were not given last-minute "hand off" cases because of the high level of stress that it would cause them. When Karla was first assigned to Major Crimes, a senior female prosecutor had warned her, "You can't ever let them see you cry or show any emotion when things get tough." This advice stuck with Karla, and she had learned to suck it up and never complain that you can't do it. Karla looked her boss in the eye, and without any begging or pleading for favors she said, "Sure, I'll take it, where's the file?"

Next she asked, "What's the date for trial?" In a monotone voice, her boss advised her it was scheduled to start in a couple of weeks. Karla turned on her forced smile and said, "That's impossible." At that point, her supervisor said, "That's why we are giving you the case." Her response was, "Great! Well, let's get started, it's soon going to be 'Showtime'."

As her boss left with a relieved look on his face, Karla wondered to herself, Why did I agree to take this case? She knew she had a calendar of more murder cases than anyone else in the Division. She had pressing speaking engagements as well as her Women Lawyers Association duties and on top of all that, her family responsibilities. She mused to herself that maybe she should have paid more attention to her mother, who tried to hammer into her pretty little head as a teenager when she had to say the word "NO."

CHAPTER 24—KARLA'S BACKGROUND

Karla had climbed the professional ladder and had reached the top rung. The Major Crimes position was reserved for the finest litigators, and she had worked her way up to that position. She had become one of the foremost experts in training prosecutors and law enforcement in the country. In the second largest city in the USA, Los Angeles, Karla was elected president of the Women Lawyers Association.

What type of background made it possible for Karla to achieve such success? What had made such an impact on her life that she would rise to such height? Could it be the fact that Karla worked as a 'Tall Nude' showgirl in Las Vegas before becoming such a talented and highly esteemed trial lawyer? One wouldn't think there was anything in common between a showgirl and lawyer. Nevertheless, Karla had learned that when it was 'Showtime,' one had to go on stage whether one felt ready or not. As she would say, "You never let the audience see you sweat."

Karla grew up in a small town in Pennsylvania and came from a loving family. Passing through adolescence had its moments, when she had to deal with her long spindly legs. In time she realized that those lanky legs made it possible for her to be a natural dancer. The more she danced the more she loved it. Finally, she finished school but didn't know what to do with her life. From all that she had read, the future for a dancer was to go to Hollywood to be discovered. She talked her mother into buying her a used car and loaning her $1000, which she promised to pay back. With only a car and the money, a young Karla headed west. She soon learned that the $1000 wasn't going to stretch all the way to Southern California, so she made a stop in Las Vegas.

In a coffee shop, she saw an advertisement for showgirl auditions. She made a call and the next day she showed up at Bally's Jubilee to try out for a role as a dancer. Bally's Jubilee was one of the first Las Vegas Strip-based burlesque shows. It started in 1981 and continued for years with only slightly minor changes to the show. The highlight is when all 85 showgirls gracefully descend the stairs to familiar musical scores. The lovely leggy ladies are clad in extravagant headpieces, dressed in costumes made from feathery fans with some of the dancers slightly overexposed in the breast area. It is a fashionable floorshow with tall gorgeous showgirls strutting their stuff with all the glitz, glamour, and elegance expected in a Vegas production.

Karla quickly realized that the naïve young lady from hometown USA had entered another world. She got up and did her dance routine with her long legs and 20-year-old figure. She felt awkward and noticed the other women were painted with makeup and dressed in a provocative manner. After the audition, a disillusioned Karla collected her bag and proceeded to leave. Someone told her to wait a minute while some of the other auditioners huddled together and gossiped about their last job.

The head person called out to her saying they had a part for her in the Jubilee Show as a "Tall Nude" dancer. This set Karla back. She was hoping for one of the orthodox dance positions. She reflected on her financial situation and her burning desire to be a dancer. She asked several unsophisticated questions like, what was the role of a "Tall Nude?" The answer was unsettling, but she needed a dancing job. It was one of those pivotal moments in one's life. The Jubilee producers needed an answer now since they had more auditions to conduct.

With a sheepish smile, the young dancer from Pennsylvania said to the Vegas producer, "Could you give me a moment to call my mother and see if it would be OK?" The producer had never heard such a request before and must have been as surprised as Karla. He said, "Sure sure." Karla ran to a phone and called her mother. She didn't know how her mother was going to react to the news. No one in her family had ever been a 'Tall Nude' dancer, or for that matter ever performed in public as a showgirl.

Karla continued to press her mother as to whether to take the showgirl position and asked what her grandmother would think of her. Her mother responded by saying, "It's a great opportunity and we just won't tell grandma about the 'Tall Nude' part." She went back to the producer and said, "OK." That began an extended career appearing as a showgirl in Bally's Jubilee.

The experience of being on stage, in front of a live audience every day gave her the confidence that she could do anything. Karla grew from a young, leggy 20-year-old girl to a worldly-wise woman within a short period of time.

After the exciting world of glitz and glitter, Karla recognized that there was more she wanted to do with her life. She had this notion of being an attorney but didn't know whether she had the discipline to make it through law school. Again, she packed her bags and headed to the San Francisco bay area, where she enrolled in law school. Her years as a showgirl put things in prospective and she excelled in law school. One summer she got a job as a law clerk at the Los Angeles DA's Office and tried out her performing talents in a courtroom. She loved it, and the DA's Office recognized she was a natural litigator. She could think fast on her feet and was never at a loss for words.

After passing the state bar exam, she went directly to the DA's office, where she quickly went to work prosecuting DUI and shoplifting cases. She was always anxious to go to trial on any type of case. She wanted to polish her skills in order to be the very best litigator in the courthouse.

(On the following page are various photos of Karla Kerlin from Showgirl to DA.)

Graphic 9

KARLA KERLIN
FROM SHOWGIRL TO DA

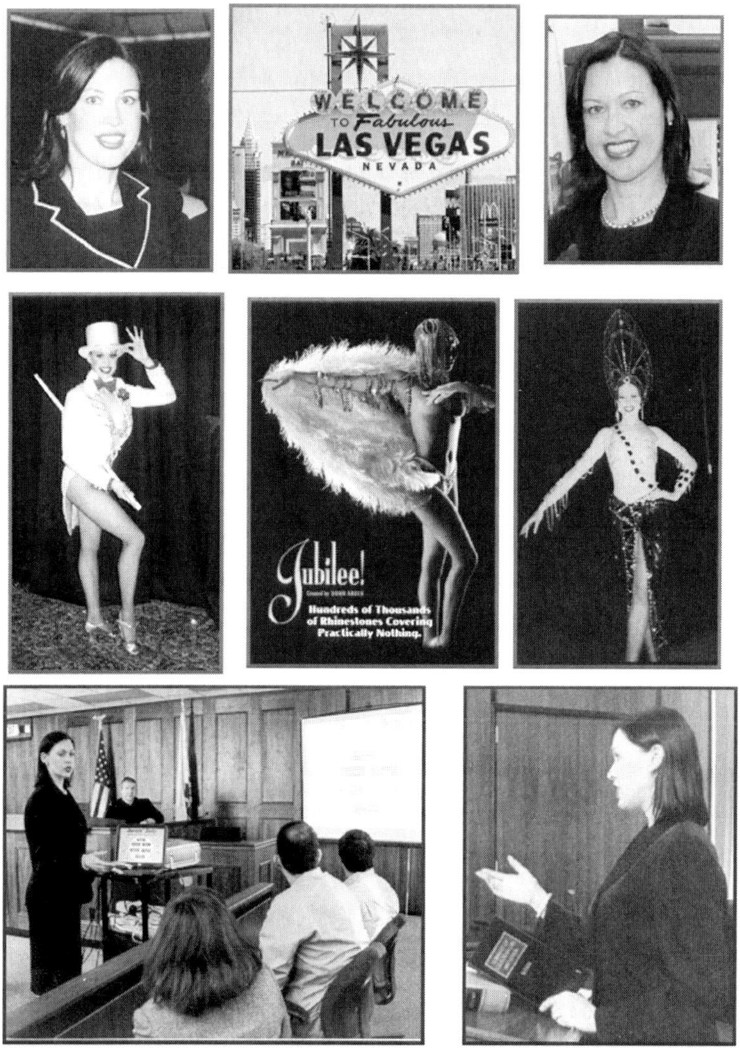

CHAPTER 25—KARLA GETTING READY FOR TRIAL

When a prosecutor is the recipient of a "hand off," the first thing to do is call the investigating officer and receive a heads up on the case. Since Karla had done the preliminary hearing on the case, she was acquainted with the FBI agents. The Elliot Ness era for the FBI had long passed when they concentrated on chasing gangsters and bootleggers. Over the years, the FBI has excelled in white-collar crimes, which are often called 'paper cases.' The FBI Agents, David Clouse and Kelly Dempsey, were truly professional and dedicated to their jobs, but the question was whether they were qualified homicide detectives.

Karla had tried numerous homicides for LAPD and LASD, and she had learned the proper procedure in finding information on a murder case. Both the LAPD and Sheriff's Department always prepared a so-called 'Murder Book,' which is divided into specific categories. It makes it easier to find things, since it contains a section for the coroner, ballistics, DNA, each witness, each victim, etc. In other words, everything is easy to find. Since the FBI doesn't specialize in murder cases, they don't use a 'Murder Book' format. The FBI tends to set up their reports in a chronological order. For a DA, this is like trying to find a needle in a haystack, since things aren't grouped by categories, but by date. Basically, you have to guess when the report was written in order to find it.

Karla's initiation into the case was that she couldn't find anything, since nothing she needed was conveniently located. The agents tried to be helpful but were baffled as to why Karla couldn't understand where things were. Karla was frustrated because she was spending so much time just trying to locate reports. Two different organizational approaches were colliding, and there wasn't the luxury of having the extra time to sort it all out. Karla started creating her own folders, grouping similar reports together so they would be easier for her to find and have at her fingertips.

She took the transcripts home and made time to read them after she had tucked her daughter into bed. Her husband picked up the slack with the home chores and she used the weekends to assimilate all the facts in the case. It was soon apparent to her how important the cellphone records were. Shane's cellphone alone could convict him. All the FBI had to do was show his cellphone was activated in the vicinity of the Afton Canyon Campground area during the early morning hours of December 3rd. Also, there were more incriminating cellphone calls in the Las Vegas area, which could be proven by the cell tower sites in that area. She immediately set up a meeting with the FBI agents to learn firsthand the answer to her questions about the case.

Karla took control of the meeting and asked to see the cell tower records of all the phone calls between Shane and Frandsen. The agents explained that they had copies of the cellphone records, but not for the cellphone tower records. Karla responded that she needed the cell tower records because it would prove beyond any doubt that the killers were together at the time of the burial, and their travel to Vegas only hours after the murders. The one FBI agent looked at Karla and said the tower records were destroyed and didn't exist anymore. He explained that cell tower records are only kept by the phone company for 90 days, and the FBI didn't get involved in the investigation of the case until 92 days had passed. So by the time the FBI got a search warrant for the cell tower records, they had all been deleted.

Karla sat back in her chair in disbelief. The strongest evidence in the case had just evaporated. After comprehending the giant hole in her case, Karla regrouped her thoughts and addressed the questions about the witnesses.

Next, Karla inquired as to the status of all the witnesses and whether they were available to testify. That was when one of the agents made a matter-of-fact announcement that one of the key witnesses had fled the country and the others refused to cooperate in the prosecution since they were friends of the defendants. As a matter of fact, most of the witnesses were hostile and resistant to any cooperation.

If that wasn't enough bad news, the other agent exclaimed that a sales clerk and a waiter who the prosecution needed as witnesses were going to torpedo the DA's case. They claimed the victims had been alive and had visited Vegas when, in fact, they were dead and buried in a deep grave in the desert. A frown came over Karla's face as she gave the agent a look of "you've got to be kidding." What had she gotten herself into?

As Karla absorbed all the bad news she thought, how could any DA convince 12 jurors to convict with so little evidence? This case wasn't sizing up as a winner but more of a loser or a hung jury at best. After a dozen years of trying cases, she knew that you win some and you lose some, no matter how hard you try. Yet, no attorney likes to lose, especially in front of their courthouse colleagues.

As though things couldn't get any worse, she learned that the judge had ruled the murder trial was to be filmed so it could be made into a documentary. Shocked and dismayed could be one way to describe Karla's reaction to the fact that the entire world, including her close friends and family, would be able to view her lose a murder case on TV. Now every word she spoke during the trial would be recorded on film, and any misstep or mispronunciation would be captured to be held in perpetuity.

The advantage for actors in movies is that they have the opportunity of having numerous takes, and then editors decide on the most effective ones to use. In a real trial, there is only one take with no repeats. What incredible pressure to be under, day after day, throughout the entire trial. Just being a trial attorney is stressful enough, but having a large TV audience looking over your shoulder can mortify even the best attorneys.

Karla gathered her thoughts and accepted the fact that she didn't have a choice. She would draw upon her past experiences as a Vegas showgirl and put on her "show face" even when everything was falling apart around her. She remembered the good old days as a showgirl having to walk down the staircase on stage with her smiling eyes fixed on the audience, who was staring at every move she made. Karla knew that when it was "Showtime" you put on the best performance ever, no matter what the problems may be.

CHAPTER 26—NEED FOR VISUAL TRIAL

Show business had taught Karla the importance of communication. You have to play to the audience. If the audience, or in her case the jurors, can't understand or comprehend the facts or the law, then you can't be successful. Karla recognized that the use of visuals was the best way to convey information to jurors. Directly after she had grasped the facts of the case, she proceeded to the DA's Trial Support Division and asked for assistance in creating some visuals that she could use in the trial.

The first visual she had made was described as the Relationship of Parties chart. Its purpose was to explain to the jury who the various parties were and their relationship to each other. Are they connected as friends or acquaintances to the others? Karla knew that if the jurors became confused as to who everyone was, they would never understand the importance of the cellphone calls between the suspects.

Karla had received word the case would be tried in Judge Susan Speer's courtroom. She had learned that this judge used a different procedure for questioning potential jurors. She had the attorneys from both sides give a mini-opening statement to all of the prospective jurors. The judge's theory was the jurors could better answer the attorneys' questions as to whether they could be fair and impartial in this particular case if they had a basic understanding of the case.

However, the judge also believed that this procedure would make the case seem more exciting so the jurors would want to serve on that specific trial. Based on the judge's experience, some jurors would try to manufacture excuses in order not to serve as a juror. If the jurors became interested in a case, they would be more willing to serve as jurors.

During the jury selection, Karla utilized her so called 'Relationship of Parties' chart to walk the potential jurors through who each of the parties was and what their involvement was in the case. She used photos of the parties with their names so the jurors could better keep track of 'who's who in the zoo.' The top square was reserved for the two defendants in the case. Even though only Shane Huang was on trial for murder in this proceeding, Karla wanted the jurors to know both Shane Huang and Frandsen were listed as defendants in the case. The bottom square included photos of both victims, Ben Wertzberger and Adar Ne'eman.

The focal point in the chart was a photo of the pink house at 7812 De Soto Avenue in Canoga Park. Karla wanted the prospective jurors to understand there were three people who were involved in the marijuana growing. Those people were Shane, who was the mastermind on the business side of the operation; Jamil Khachatouian, who was the expert in setting up the facility to grow the marijuana; and finally, Ben Wertzberger, who was in charge of the daily operation of maintaining the plants and harvesting the marijuana. Karla used a triangle that connected Shane to Ben, to a photo of Jamil Khachatouian, filled in with the words, "Marijuana Business."

The other key players in the case would be called as witnesses by the prosecution. On the left side of Khachatouian, Karla placed the name Joe Pierson, since she would be calling him as a witness to describe to the jury the events leading up to the murders. His connection to all these people was that he was a friend of Khachatouian, who was one of the partners in the marijuana business. Then on the right side of the chart, Karla listed the name of Nick Tuttle, who was a close friend of the other defendant Frandsen. Tuttle would be the most crucial witness for Karla, since he was with the victims for almost 10 hours when they were being held captive by Shane. The one remaining player was Ora Vodnoy, whose name was placed next to Tuttle. She was involved in making the phone calls to the victims' relatives in Israel. These were the main players the jurors would have to know about and keep straight in their minds. Besides using this 'Relationship of Parties' chart in her mini-opening statement, during jury selection she would reuse it in her actual Opening Statement as well as in her Argument at the end of the case.

Karla would have the various witnesses refer to this chart when they were explaining whom they were talking about. Karla had the chart marked as an exhibit so the jury could use it during their deliberations. What that chart didn't explain was the time that key events transpired in the case. It was essential for the jury to keep in mind the important dates that occurred during the crime and during the investigation. The criminal events happened over a nine-day period. But it was also important that the jury understand the various stages of the investigation that occurred during 2003.

The case had built in confusion. For one thing, there had been three separate search warrants served on the pink house. The **first** was on April 8th , and was specifically restricted to looking for evidence of the marijuana growing. The **second** was on September 12th; this warrant was focused on finding weapons and large sums of money. And the **third** search warrant was on October 1st, specifically looking for the "Star Shoes" that Shane bought at the Catwalk Store in Vegas.

Another fact that was confusing was the search for the victims' bodies in the desert on September 21st. In most murder cases, the body is found first and the investigation is conducted afterwards. This case is an example of how important it was for the jury to understand the sequence of events. Karla created a simple timeline with a short statement explaining each event. However, Karla realized it was too wordy and hard to convey the amount of time that transpired between events. After several drafts, she decided to use the "Box" Timeline that helped the jurors compartmentalize in their minds the various key events.

One of the messages she wanted to give to the jury was to always be conscious of the fact that there had been 10 months between the murders and finding the bodies. Also, it was important for the prosecution to illustrate why it wasn't able to obtain the information from the phone companies regarding the phone tower sites for each of the calls. This chart showed that the FBI wasn't contacted until February and that the first search warrant wasn't issued until April. That was more than the 90 days, which was the amount of time the phone companies kept their records regarding the tower sites of cell phone calls.

When Karla was preparing her "Box" Timeline, she realized that there were so many details that she needed to explain to the jury. It was imperative the jurors be able to comprehend when the crucial cellphone calls were made. She experimented by preparing a "Clock Timeline." This worked well for the first 12 hours. But in this case, the killings occurred during the early morning hours of December 3rd. Since there were so many entries, the visual seemed to be confusing in and of itself. Then it was decided to use various colors to distinguish the cellphone calls, as well as differentiate these calls from actual meetings of the parties.

It became apparent to Karla that she would need three separate "Clock Timeline" charts for the various 12-hour periods such as: Monday p.m., Tuesday a.m., and later Tuesday p.m. when the defendants were in Las Vegas. The next two 'Clock Timelines' were marked as exhibits and went into the jury room. During deliberation, the jurors could see the big gap between 1:46 a.m. to 4:57 a.m. Karla argued that was the time in which the murders occurred, as well as the clean-up of the crime scene.

After explaining the clock timelines, Karla knew the next part of her Opening Statement had to be where all the events occurred. She knew the easiest way to visualize all the locations was to use a map. This would show the relative distances between the various locations and orient the jurors to the location of the Afton Canyon Campground. Many people confuse the two small communities of Barstow and Baker. It is easy to mix up which comes first. This map helped the jurors visualize that the campground was midway between the two desert cities.

Everyone driving to Las Vegas has sped by the campground turnoff without paying any attention to the exit. It was important in Karla's case that the jurors understand that anyone traveling from Los Angeles to Las Vegas would have a perfect opportunity to use the Afton Canyon Campground as a place to bury the bodies. The map illustrated how close the freeway was to the gravesite.

(On the following pages are the exhibits of the Relation of Parties as well as the three different clock Timelines.)

Graphic 10

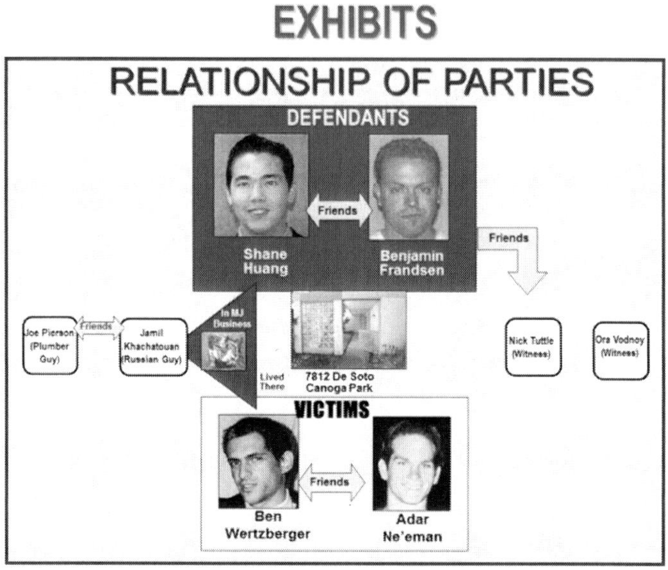
EXHIBITS
RELATIONSHIP OF PARTIES
DEFENDANTS
Friends
Shane Huang
Benjamin Frandsen
Friends
Joe Pierson (Plumber Guy)
Friends
Jamil Khachatouan (Russian Guy)
In MJ Business
Lived There
7812 De Soto Canoga Park
Nick Tuttle (Witness)
Ora Vodnoy (Witness)
VICTIMS
Friends
Ben Wertzberger
Adar Ne'eman

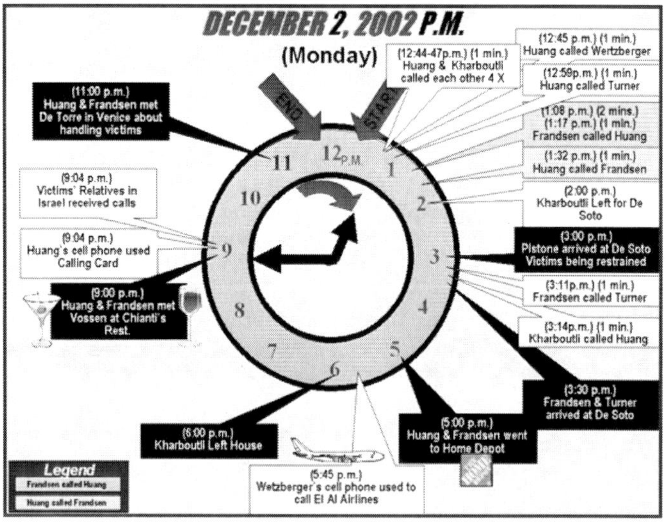
DECEMBER 2, 2002 P.M.
(Monday)
END
START
12 P.M.
(12:44-47p.m.) (1 min.) Huang & Kharboutli called each other 4 X
(12:45 p.m.) (1 min.) Huang called Wertzberger
(12:59p.m.) (1 min.) Huang called Turner
(1:08 p.m.) (2 mins.) (1:17 p.m.) (1 min.) Frandsen called Huang
(1:32 p.m.) (1 min.) Huang called Frandsen
(2:00 p.m.) Kharboutli Left for De Soto
(3:00 p.m.) Pistone arrived at De Soto Victims being restrained
(3:11p.m.) (1 min.) Frandsen called Turner
(3:14p.m.) (1 min.) Kharboutli called Huang
(3:30 p.m.) Frandsen & Turner arrived at De Soto
(5:00 p.m.) Huang & Frandsen went to Home Depot
(5:45 p.m.) Wetzberger's cell phone used to call El Al Airlines
(6:00 p.m.) Kharboutli Left House
(9:00 p.m.) Huang & Frandsen met Vossen at Chianti's Rest.
(9:04 p.m.) Huang's cell phone used Calling Card
(9:04 p.m.) Victims' Relatives in Israel received calls
(11:00 p.m.) Huang & Frandsen met De Torre in Venice about handling victims
Legend
Frandsen called Huang
Huang called Frandsen

CHAPTER 27—THE TRIAL

Karla had learned firsthand from her previous trials that the Opening Statement can be a critical stage for a case. It occurs immediately after the jury selection is completed. The jurors are anxious to learn more about this case and are particularly receptive to listening to both sides. She suggested to the jurors that her Opening Statement was like a road map explaining where they are going, what they are going to see, what things are important, and what it all means. Karla knew the actual trial of this case would be extremely disjointed since many of the witnesses would be called out of order. Because some of the witnesses were coming from long distances, such as Israel and Nevada, she would not be able to call them to the witness stand in a logical order. She had to have ready to testify enough witnesses to fill an entire court day. She knew that judges become cranky when the attorneys run out of witnesses and the court has to take an early recess for the rest of the day.

What makes the logistics of trial scheduling so difficult is there is no way to predict how long the cross-examination will take. A defense attorney may decide to spend hours attacking one of the prosecution's witnesses. Other times, they may not even ask a single question of the prosecution witness. Witnesses also get grouchy if they are called to court and sit around all day and then are told to come back the next day.

Karla had learned that there was no way to precisely know how many witnesses to inconvenience by having them come to the courthouse and sit and wait. She had come up with a strategy of reserving the testimony of the investigating officers, who always have to be present in court. When she inadvertently runs out of witnesses, she calls the investigating officer to fill in for the rest of the day. This makes the judge happy but confuses the jurors to no end, since the detectives' testimony doesn't fit in neatly with the previous witnesses. That's why Karla spends considerable time during her Opening Statement explaining how the witnesses' testimony joins together. In that way, the jurors have a way of compartmentalizing where to place in their minds the testimony of the witness who is called out of order.

On April 27, 2005, Karla called her first witness, Lillian Roberts (Pseudonym), the owner of the DeSoto house in Canoga Park. She testified that she had rented the house to Shane Huang and Jamil Khachatouian, and that somehow Ben Wertzberger's name was added to the lease since he was the one who would actually be living in the house. She indicated that Shane always paid the rent on time to her so she never had to visit the property to check things out.

The next witness was Krista Autry, who was Ben's girlfriend and in fact had moved in with Ben at the DeSoto house. She testified she wasn't comfortable living in a marijuana-growing house and after a month she moved out. She praised her boyfriend, Ben, as being exceptionally creative in his quest to be a professional DJ.

Karla wanted to get Ben's friends out of the way, so she first put on Doran Koller, who was the first person Ben contacted when he came to the United States. Ben lived with him for a short time at his house in Porter Ranch, which is in the northern part of the San Fernando Valley. Later Ben moved to the Hollywood area to be closer to his work. The only other thing he added was the fact that Ben and Adar stayed with him for a couple of days just before they disappeared. He remembered Ben mentioning that he had to repay someone for a phone bill he owed.

Then Karla called Joseph Pierson, the so called 'Plumber Guy,' to the witness stand. She established that he was a friend of Jamil Khachatouian and that he had helped set up the lighting and water apparatus for growing the marijuana. He testified that on December 2nd Jamil got a call from Shane to come help him because he had caught Ben and someone else breaking into the De Soto house. He finished up his work and by 3:00 p.m. arrived at the pink house and noticed Ben and another guy, Adar, were restrained on the sofa in the living room. Also present was Jamil, and later, around 3:30 p.m., Frandsen and Tuttle arrived. Shane was yelling and threatening the victims with a long sword. He was trying to encourage Ben to pay back what he had taken from his place.

At one point, Pierson spat on Ben in order to help Shane put pressure on Ben to pay up. He explained that around 5:00 p.m., Shane and Frandsen left to go to Home Depot, and when they returned they had a shovel, rope, and some large bags. Pierson was there when Shane asked if anyone had a problem if he killed the two guys.

Karla asked Pierson questions about being wired by the FBI in an attempt to tape-record Shane making incriminating statements. Pierson testified that on one occasion, when he was wearing the recording device, Shane did admit that he went to Home Depot and did come back with a shovel and some rope. When Pierson asked what he should say to the FBI agents who were attempting to question him, Shane said, "I would appreciate it if you would lie to them." Karla needed Pierson to authenticate the tape of those incriminating statements. This would allow the tape to be an exhibit to which the jurors could listen to during their deliberations.

Karla knew what was going to happen on cross, so she tried to soften the blow by asking if he, Pierson, had given any different statements. She was hoping he would explain that he didn't want to get his friend in trouble as the reason for being less than candid with the agents in the initial stages of the investigation. He gave a short explanation and Karla stated, "The People have no further questions of this witness." At that moment the defense attorney nearly jumped out of his seat and starting to show all the inconsistent statements that Pierson had made over all the months. The cross-examination was not a pretty sight for the prosecution as Brooklier caught Pierson in one lie after another.

Karla never thought the cross would end, as her witness was becoming testier with the defense attorney. All Pierson could think of was, "When is this all going to end?" There was nothing Karla could do to plug up the credibility holes of her key witness.

Eventually, it was over and Karla hurriedly called as her next witness the Coroner, Dr. Steven Trenkle. His testimony was a 'piece of cake' after Pierson's. She was able to get the coroner to testify that Adar had been struck in the neck and the force of the fractured neck bone caused the victim to be unable to breathe. All this testimony went well, and even the cross-examination didn't damage the People's case.

Next to take the witness stand was Charles Denton, which Karla knew would be like pulling teeth. He was a chummy friend of Shane's, and he didn't want to say anything that would hurt his pal. He admitted that Shane and Frandsen came to his house after the Monday night football game. He testified that Shane wanted advice as to what he should do to someone who had burglarized his place. His suggestion was to "fuck them up and then let them go." Even though it was clear that he wasn't telling all, it was important to get him to establish that the visit was moments before the crucial phone call Shane made to Shane's UCLA buddy.

On May 3rd Karla called the custodian of records from the Sprint Phone Company. He would authenticate the cellphone records of all the parties in the case. As mundane as this testimony seemed, it would be crucial in providing the corroboration of Pierson and Tuttle's testimony. It would also illustrate how Shane and Frandsen were always calling each other, except for the times they were together killing the victims and when they were digging the grave.

The two mothers were the following witnesses. A translator was used, so the questioning went very slowly. The mothers made good witnesses as to how they had learned their sons were missing. They gave the jury insight as to how difficult it had been to get any agency to investigate their missing sons' disappearance.

CHAPTER 28—MORE WITNESSES

The next witness to be called was Coleen Rauh, who had to be the most surprising witness that Karla had called. Karla had no idea how well she would do on the witness stand. She worked as a 'tow truck coordinator' for vehicles that had been parked too long in the Las Vegas metropolitan area. On December 7th she was dispatched to 8th and Fremont Streets to tow away Ben's car. She noticed the numerous parking tickets on the windshield. She looked inside and was surprised to find the keys to the car in the ignition and a wallet was on the seat. Also, there was a calendar organizer containing airline tickets from NY to Israel, as well as some credit cards. She continued testifying that the car was parked next to the police annex where officers came and went. She related that luggage filled the interior of the car, making it impossible for anyone but the driver to be seated. Looking through the rear windows, one could see an Alesis amplifier and a Toshiba laptop, as well as recording equipment.

Karla was impressed how sharp she was as to every detail. She asked her if she could calculate when the car was parked at that location. Witness Rauh said that she had reviewed all the records of the parking Enforcement Officers working in that area on December 3rd, and the vehicle was parked, or became out of compliance, with the meter between 4:43 p.m. and 6:41p.m., when the first ticket was written.

She had supplied Karla with photos of the location with her city van, parked where Ben's Chevrolet had been parked. Karla used the photos in her questioning and had her explain each one of them. The jurors became immersed in her answers. She was incredibly professional and thoroughly prepared. By asking her those questions, Karla had nailed down the exact time range when Ben's car was parked at that location. That disproved the theory that Ben and Adar had gone about the town using Adar's credit card. How could they do that if their only means of transportation was a car that had been parked before 6:41p.m? The other fact that Karla had proven was that someone had planted the car at that location, since the keys were in ignition and all their property was on the seats. All that was missing was a sign saying 'Steal Me.' Coleen Rauh was a remarkable witness that attorneys can only dream of.

Karla was pleasantly surprised, but now she had to move on to the next witness, Eagle Parks, from the Catwalk store in Las Vegas. Karla had to call her to prove that Adar's credit card was used in Vegas. Parks testified that two men came in on December 3rd around 7:42 p.m. and purchased two pairs of velour pants, several shirts, and a pair of Demonia shoes totaling $467.87. She indicated that the person primarily involved with the purchase could be described as a little bit overweight, with curly brownish hair and light eyes. Karla asked her if she requested any form of identification, which she indicated that she had. The man showed her a passport for his 'ID' which she looked at it and said, "That doesn't look like you." She commented, that the man laughed and said he had changed his hair. She continued to put the sale through and it was accepted.

Later in her testimony, she was asked to identify the customers. She identified a photo of Frandsen as being the larger man with the curly hair. However, as to the other man, he was taller and thinner but she wasn't able to identify him.

Karla knew that Brooklier was just waiting to cross-examine this witness because he hoped that she would identify Ben and Adar. So Karla tried to soften the blow by indicating that the PIs, as well as the victims' mothers, had shown her photos of the victims. That might explain why the witness had identified the other purchaser as one of the Israeli young men.

Brooklier knew how to get what he wanted from this witness, so his cross-examination wasn't as long as Karla had anticipated. She had run out of witnesses, so she plugged in one of the investigators to finish out the day. Agent David Kidd was called to testify about the search warrants, starting with the **first** one issued on April 8, 2003. He described the two marijuana-growing rooms—hidden behind a false wall with a mirror for a secret door—in which the watering and lighting systems were set up.

He was also asked about the **second** search warrant, issued on September 12th 2003, when a Katana, often referred to as a Samurai sword, was recovered. Also recovered was $10,000 in cash. Then there was a **third** search warrant, issued on October 1st, in which a pair of Shasha fine shoes were seized. Karla used Agent Kidd to describe the search for the grave. He stated that he was a Forensic Anthropologist and explained the process of finding and removing the corpses from the grave. This was typical CSI material that jurors eat up, so Karla felt that this testimony went well. She followed this with the testimony of Agent David Clouse, followed by Agent Kelly Dempsey, who walked the jurors through all of the investigation they had conducted.

The next challenging witness was Ora Vodnoy. Karla didn't know what she would say. She was a good friend of Shane and didn't want to say anything to hurt him. Yet she had said enough to the agents, in which she admitted being involved in and making the phone calls to the victims' families to check that Shane had their correct addresses. Since she had originally been arrested by the FBI for aiding and abetting, she was hostile to anyone who had anything to do with the government. Karla knew how hard it was going to be to guide her through the phone calls, but she was locked into what Vodnoy had told the FBI. The word 'hostile' does not truly describe her contempt for Karla and the FBI.

On May 5th Karla called her last witness, David Sherwood, Shane's UCLA buddy who was working with him on their MBA project. He didn't want to testify against Shane, so he was going to volunteer anything he thought might be helpful for Shane. All Karla needed out of him was admitting to receiving a phone call from Shane in which he said, "An emergency had come up and I have to leave town." Although Sherwood tried to be vague, Karla pinned him down. She had the phone records showing that he received a phone call from Shane around 10:30 p.m. Even with the lack of cooperation from him, Karla was able to get him to provide the information needed.

She couldn't believe she had gone through all her witnesses in five days. So many of the civilian witnesses didn't want to be in court, and extracting testimony from them wasn't easy. Then it was time for Brooklier to call the defense witnesses. Karla didn't know what to expect from the defense witnesses.

The defense commenced with their first witness, Michael Gates (Pseudonym), the former waiter from the Outback Steakhouse in Las Vegas. Brooklier led him through the date of December 3rd 2003, around 10:00 p.m. when he was working as a waiter.

A young lady came in and sat at one of the dining tables. A short time later, a young man arrived and they both ordered dinner. At the end of dinner they used a credit card to pay their bill. The name on the card was Adar Ne'eman. Gates asked for identification and compared it to the credit card. Seeing that they matched, he continued to process the credit card and returned it. He described the male as being European looking, with a thin build. Some five months later, the FBI showed him a photo lineup where he picked out Adar Ne'eman's photo as the male customer.

On her cross-examination, Karla had to do a surgical strike on one point and get this witness off the stand. She started by asking about the man's description. Didn't you tell the agents that the man was wearing tortoise shell rimmed glasses? He agreed that he had told the agents that. She asked him if he always asked for a diner's identification when a patron uses a credit card. He said he always checked a person's photo ID on all credit card transactions. Karla stepped back from the witness stand stating, "Are you sure? I have never been asked for an ID when using a credit card in a restaurant." She turned abruptly and walked to her chair curtly stating, "No more questions of this witness, your Honor."

The next witness could be just as damming for Karla. The defense called Tara Emerson, the other sales clerk from the Catwalk store. The bailiff escorted this witness to the stand and she was asked if she remembered the purchase of the two velour pants and the Demonia shoes. She looked at the receipt and said she was present although it was another salesperson's transaction. Then she was asked to describe the two males. She remembered one was a bigger white guy, curly hair and acted flamboyant. He was the one making the purchase of the items. The other guy looked more Middle Eastern but she said she couldn't identify him.

Brooklier was trying to get her to identify Adar as the second person. Then he asked her if she identified a specific photo when the FBI showed her a six-pack lineup. She admitted that she had indicated that the photo of Adar looked similar to the person. She claimed she never told the agent that she was absolutely certain that was the other purchaser. Brooklier tried to get her to identify Adar's photo but she continued to say she was uncertain.

As to the identification of the person making the purchase, she had no difficulty in identifying Frandsen. Brooklier wanted to finish strong, so he asked her if either of the two men looked Asian. This witness said that according to her recollection neither man looked Asian.

In listening to the witness's testimony, Karla realized she gave the impression the two young men were some type of tourists. She got the witness to say, "They said they were from out of town, they were staying at a hotel. And they asked us to go out with them that night." This was a gift to Karla, because now she could argue that the two men sounded more like Shane and Frandsen since **they were staying in a hotel**. She would tell the jury that if it had been Ben and Adar, they would have said they were staying with a friend. She was pleased that this witness had backed off her identification of Adar. The identification of Frandsen was solid, so she asked few questions on cross, but that was all she needed.

The next defense witness was Jason Bell, the person who was involved with the sale of $8,000 worth of computer equipment at Best Buy. Brooklier asked him how many persons were involved in the purchase. He replied, "Three." The defense attorney asked if he ever identified any of the parties. He indicated that the FBI showed him a photo lineup and he picked the photo of number 4, which was Frandsen's photo. He said he could not identify any of the others. However, since it was such a large purchase he asked for two forms of identification. One was a passport in the name of the credit card holder, which was Adar Ne'eman. For some reason, the bank rejected the sale, and the salesman told the men to come back later.

Brooklier was reaching the end of his witnesses. One was a professor from UCLA Business School, who indicated that Shane should have been in class on December 4th, since that was an important lecture date. But no one actually took attendance. So that witness was of limited value for the defense. However, it was a way for the Brooklier to present evidence showing that Shane was working for his MBA.

CHAPTER 29—SHOULD SHANE TESTIFY?

All the courtroom watchers in the audience had been waiting for the big moment when Shane would take the witness stand to tell his story as to what happened. The defense had tried to spin the facts to make it appear that Shane had not gone to Las Vegas. Their position laid the blame on Frandsen as the person who committed the murders and that Shane had nothing to do with it. The best way to sell that theory would be by having Shane testify. In that way, he could explain to the jury his story that he wasn't present during the killings and that he never buried the bodies or even traveled to Las Vegas afterwards.

What the defense had to consider was how well Shane could articulate his position when testifying in front of the jury. By the time of his arrest, the defendant had graduated with his Master's Degree from the UCLA Anderson School of Business. In September of 2003, he had an excellent position in one of the top companies in the area. There was no doubt that Shane was bright enough as well as sufficiently articulate to convey his story.

However, Brooklier had to consider how well Shane would hold up under the intense cross-examination by a strong litigator like Karla. Some defendants can keep their wits about them when they are asked pointed question by the prosecutor. Other defendants will try to be too clever in answering the hard questions. They often dig a bigger hole for themselves and find themselves being buried in that bottomless pit. Shane had always been able to talk his way out of difficult situations, as he did when the detectives originally interrogated him about the killings. Shane thought he could handle any type of situation. The question that Brooklier had to decide was whether Shane on the witness stand would appear as a confident, believable person or a cocky, lying killer.

Throughout the trial, Shane was advising his attorney what to say and do. His defense attorney was highly skilled and didn't need any advice from his client as to how to try the case. Shane's attitude during the trial was that he was so smart that he was going to 'beat the rap.' Throughout the trial, when Karla was having difficulty with the prosecution witnesses, Shane would smile or appear to gloat at her plight. This snickering didn't go unnoticed by the court watchers and possibly the jurors.

After the few defense witnesses had testified and the defense was about ready to Rest its case, the defense attorney had to provide that crucial advice to his client whether to testify or not. Brooklier advised Shane that it would be best for him not to testify. Shane seemed to be in disagreement with that advice. Out of the presences of the jury, the judge asked Shane directly whether he wanted to testify. He responded to the judge by saying, "I want to testify, but I will follow the advice of my attorney and not testify." The judge restated the question, telling him that he had a right to testify if he wanted to. He again indicated that he wanted to but his attorney had advised against it.

Then Shane and the judge had a clash in which they both went around and around regarding whether to testify or not. Karla couldn't wait to get Shane on the witness stand. She was rooting for Shane to testify. Shane's story was vulnerable since he would have difficulty convincing the jury that he had nothing to do with the killings or the trip to Las Vegas. The prosecution wanted him to try to explain why he told Tuttle that he was talking to him on his cellphone from inside the casino if he never went to Vegas. There were so many areas where Shane was vulnerable if he took the witness stand.

As the judge was questioning Shane about testifying, the defense attorney had to be hoping that he would just say "no," that he didn't want to testify. After several more attempts, Shane finally said that he would not be taking the witness stand. Defense counsel Brooklier had to be greatly relieved. At the same time, Karla recognized that the jury would never see what a devious and untruthful individual Shane really was. If she had been able to cross-examine him, the jurors would have seen another side of Shane, one which would project a cocky, arrogant individual who was capable of murder.

The defense then 'Rested' and after several formalities the case was set for Argument. It was Thursday and the case had gone on for several weeks. The judge excused the jury and told them to come back for Argument on Monday morning. The judge set Friday afternoon for both attorneys to discuss the jury instructions. On Thursday night, Karla collected all her notes and started preparing the various points she wanted to cover in her Argument. Before the trial had started, Karla had worked on some drafts of possible charts that she planned to use in her Argument. Looking through her Argument folder, she found the drafts and modified them to conform to the witnesses' testimony that had been elicited during the trial.

As Karla worked on her Argument, she tried to figure out what would be the most effective way to divide up what she would use in her Argument and what she would use in her Rebuttal Argument. Although she had never tried a case with Brooklier, she had a good idea what he would cover in his Argument. She knew that he would attack the credibility of her two key witnesses, Pierson and Tuttle. She decided that it would be better for her to use her Rebuttal Argument to show that those two witnesses were corroborated by other evidence.

CHAPTER 30—KARLA'S ARGUMENT

As a communicator, Karla recognized the advantage of using a PowerPoint slide show during the Argument phase. However, Karla's trial experience had taught her that if she used charts during her presentation of the evidence, she could get them marked as evidence, and then they would be available for the jurors to view and use during their deliberation. This was important in this particular case since it was vital for the jurors to know exactly when each phone call was made between Shane and Frandsen. As a result, Karla decided to forgo any PowerPoint slide show and concentrate on the charts, diagrams, and maps that had become exhibits.

Karla, wearing her *LA Law* business attire, stood tall and looked directly into the eyes of the jurors. Her showgirl skills had taught her to hold her head up high and ignore the TV cameras, which were capturing every move she made and word she spoke. Karla started out saying there are two types of cases: "What is it? And the other one is Who done it?" She said that this case was the latter type of case.

She had a job to do, which was explaining what the facts were and what law the jurors needed to follow. She started discussing that there are two ways you can prove **First Degree Murder**. The first way is when the killing was premeditated and deliberate. The second way is what is called the **'Felony Murder rule.'** This is when a person intends to commit a certain felony crime—such as in this case kidnapping—and during the commission of this crime someone is killed. The killing could be accidental or totally unintended, but the results would still be First Degree Murder.

Karla had to rely on the Felony Murder rule to convict Shane. She had to stress that the moving of Ben and Adar from the car to the inside of the house was a **kidnapping**. The law requires that the movement has to be for a substantial distance. The idea is that the movement in some way increases the risk of harm to the victim. The question was whether the jury would find the movement, making up the kidnapping, was for a substantial distance (the movement of Ben and Adar from Ben's car to the inside of the De Soto house.) There was no question that Shane had kept the victims in false imprisonment for many hours. However, that was not one of the felonies that qualify under the Felony Murder Rule.

Karla had to discuss the **'Aiding and Abetting'** legal concept. She explained that persons involved in committing a crime are referred to as 'Principals' in that crime. They come in two types: those who directly and actively commit the crime; and those who aid and abet the crime. In the eyes of the law both are equally guilty.

Karla's last referral to the law was in regard to '**Motive.'** She explained that the prosecution didn't have to prove a motive for the crime. However, motive could be used to prove guilt. In this case, who had a motive to be angry at Ben? It was Shane's marijuana and money that had been stolen. He thought Ben had burglarized his place two days earlier, therefore he had a motive to get even with Ben.

Karla moved on with her Argument by discussing each one of her visual aids. She started with the **Linear Timeline** and placed it on the easel. On the left hand side, she talked about all the critical dates showing when Adar arrived in LA. Then she pointed out all the events that occurred on December 2nd and 3rd, especially the actions that occurred in Las Vegas. Then she used the Timeline to give perspective as to when the FBI got involved in the case, which was three months after the crime. The chart covered almost an entire year and showed when the three search warrants were served. Ultimately, it concluded in the month of September, when the suspects were arrested and the bodies found in the desert.

Karla's presentation was smooth and seamless. With her Timeline of Events chart she was able to do what all effective communicators do, which is tell the audience three times the facts. First you tell them what you are going to tell them; second you actually tell them the facts; and third you tell them what you told them. Here Karla had used this Timeline chart three times. First, in her Opening Statement, then secondly when the jurors heard the witnesses testify to the facts, and thirdly when Karla used it in her Argument.

Next she placed on her easel the **'Clock Timeline'** for the period from noon to midnight on December 2nd. It had all the phone calls made among the various parties as well as the time when the people arrived at the house where Shane was holding the victims. Then it showed when they went to Home Depot to get a shovel and some rope, and when they left to have Ora Vodnoy make the phone calls to the victims' families in Israel. What this visual did was give the jurors an idea of the amount of time between events.

The next visual that Karla discussed was the most important in the entire case. It was the **'Clock Timeline'**, which included the period from midnight to noon on December 3rd. This visual graphically showed how Shane and Frandsen were constantly calling each other when they weren't in each other's company. The only time when there were no phone calls between them was from 1:46 a.m. to 4:57 a.m., from which, Karla said, the jurors could infer Shane and Frandsen were killing the victims and cleaning up the house before leaving with the bodies.

After that time, they resumed calling each other again since they were driving in separate cars to Las Vegas. Then at 5:45 a.m. the phone calls abruptly ceased until 8:00 a.m. Karla told the jurors that they could infer they were digging the grave to bury the bodies. Only this chart could graphically show the jurors what was going on. Karla knew that words alone couldn't describe what the cellphone calls revealed. But Karla went one step further, knowing that not all jurors would be able to remember the importance of the cellphone calls between them. During the trial, Karla had the witnesses use the chart, so it got marked as an exhibit. All those charts became exhibits and went into the jury room during deliberations.

Karla wanted the jurors to see when Shane definitely had decided to kill the victims. She wanted them to see that Shane went to talk to Denton, who came into court and testified that he told Shane to "Fuck those guys up and let them go." But could he have said something stronger? Karla wanted the jurors to see that immediately after they left Denton's place, Shane called his business-school buddy and told him that he had to go out of town. Karla argued to the jury, "So it is a reasonable inference that this was the call he was going out of town. And what is the significance of this? This suggests that after seeing Mr. Denton for whatever advice that the plan was to harm the victims fatally because they knew they were going to have to go out of town."

Karla continued to go through the remainder of her visuals, which graphically explained the testimony of all the witnesses. Then she got to Pierson's recording in which he was trying to get Shane to admit to the crime. Karla read from the transcript:

Pierson: ... I mean I saw you with the shovel and shit and all that.

Shane: Dude

Pierson: What do you mean, dude? I mean come on.

Shane: You're right. You did. You're right. You did.

Karla felt very strongly that Shane's statement was very telling and wanted to leave that with the jury. Karla concluded, "The People would ask that after you review all of the evidence in this case that you return verdicts of guilty as to both counts of First Degree Murder and that you find the special circumstance allegation of multiple murders to be true."

(On the following graphic page are the Clock Timelines)

Graphic 11

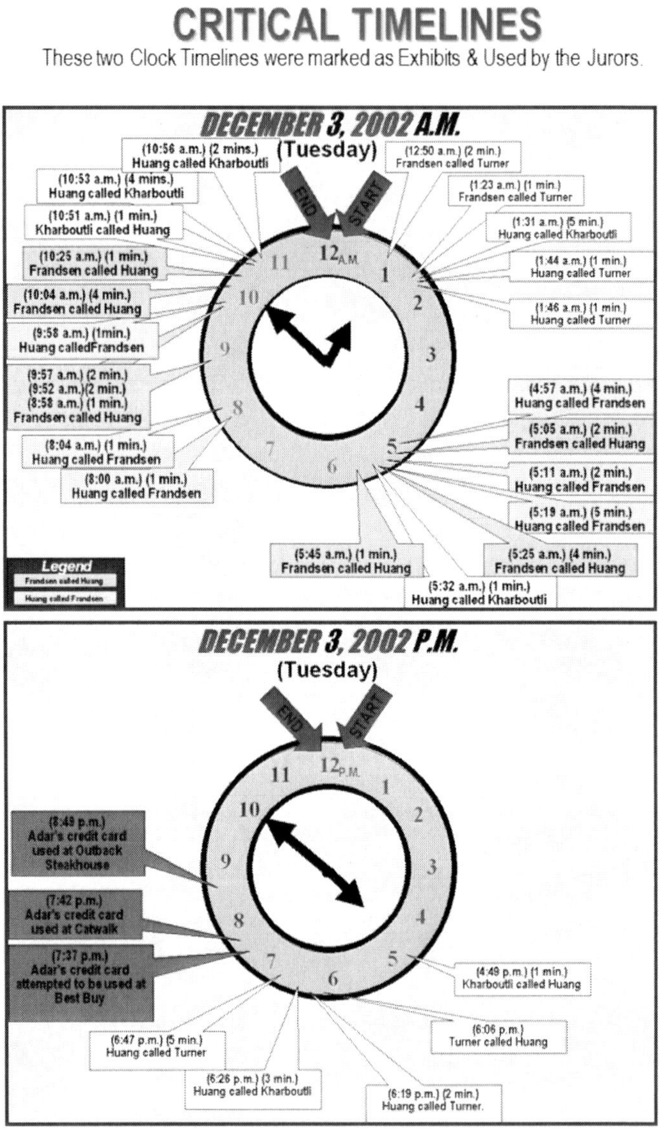
CRITICAL TIMELINES
These two Clock Timelines were marked as Exhibits & Used by the Jurors.
DECEMBER 3, 2002 A.M.
(Tuesday)
END
START
(10:56 a.m.) (2 mins.) Huang called Kharboutli
(10:53 a.m.) (4 mins.) Huang called Kharboutli
(10:51 a.m.) (1 min.) Kharboutli called Huang
(10:25 a.m.) (1 min.) Frandsen called Huang
(10:04 a.m.) (4 min.) Frandsen called Huang
(9:58 a.m.) (1min.) Huang calledFrandsen
(9:57 a.m.) (2 min.) (9:52 a.m.)(2 min.) (8:58 a.m.) (1 min.) Frandsen called Huang
(8:04 a.m.) (1 min.) Huang called Frandsen
(8:00 a.m.) (1 min.) Huang called Frandsen
(12:50 a.m.) (2 min.) Frandsen called Turner
(1:23 a.m.) (1 min.) Frandsen called Turner
(1:31 a.m.) (5 min.) Huang called Kharboutli
(1:44 a.m.) (1 min.) Huang called Turner
(1:46 a.m.) (1 min.) Huang called Turner
(4:57 a.m.) (4 min.) Huang called Frandsen
(5:05 a.m.) (2 min.) Frandsen called Huang
(5:11 a.m.) (2 min.) Huang called Frandsen
(5:19 a.m.) (5 min.) Huang called Frandsen
(5:25 a.m.) (4 min.) Frandsen called Huang
(5:45 a.m.) (1 min.) Frandsen called Huang
(5:32 a.m.) (1 min.) Huang called Kharboutli
12 A.M.
Legend
DECEMBER 3, 2002 P.M.
(Tuesday)
END
START
12 P.M.
(8:49 p.m.) Adar's credit card used at Outback Steakhouse
(7:42 p.m.) Adar's credit card used at Catwalk
(7:37 p.m.) Adar's credit card attempted to be used at Best Buy
(4:49 p.m.) (1 min.) Kharboutli called Huang
(6:06 p.m.) Turner called Huang
(6:47 p.m.) (5 min.) Huang called Turner
(6:26 p.m.) (3 min.) Huang called Kharboutli
(6:19 p.m.) (2 min.) Huang called Turner.

CHAPTER 31—DEFENSE ARGUMENT

The defense attorney was one of the best that money could buy. He was smooth but firmly aggressive, knowing how to attack the weaknesses in the prosecution's case. He started out by criticizing Karla for using so many poster board charts. He said, "She puts facts on a board—on a poster as if they are the gospel ... She wants you to believe just because it's on a poster ... This is prosecution by poster board."

After attacking Karla's visual presentation, he proceeded to zero in on the prosecution's weakness, which was relying on the testimony of Pierson and Tuttle. From the beginning of the investigation, these witnesses had tried to protect themselves, or others, by telling the FBI agents one story after another. The defense wanted to expose these inconsistencies and plant in the minds of the jurors that these witnesses were outright liars. Brooklier used these words to describe Pierson and Tuttle. He said to the jurors, "You could probably spend the next 30 years in this courthouse ... and you will never see two nut jobs like this, two more incredible liars than these people."

He showed how Pierson told different stories to Agent Clouse and if the agents made suggestions as to what they would like to know, Pierson would repeat that version. The defense's biggest criticism of Pierson was that he waited until the time of trial to tell the agents that Shane said, "He was going to kill these people." Brooklier tried to show that Pierson would say things so he wouldn't be prosecuted for the role he played in the holding and imprisonment of these victims.

The defense then tried to give an explanation as to why Shane went to all the trouble of having Ora Vodnoy make the calls to the victims' relatives. The defense's response was that Shane was looking for an 'exit strategy' as to letting the victims go. When he talked to Denton he was looking for a way out. The defense suggested that Shane was angry with Ben because he thought he had stolen from him, but after holding them against their will, he wanted to find a way to release them. His fear was that they would report him to the police for the false imprisonment and the fact that he was growing marijuana in the De Soto house. The defense's question to the jurors was "Why would a guy going for an MBA kill two people over $5,000 worth of marijuana? This didn't make sense."

Then the defense wanted to explain the incriminating tape Pierson recorded of Shane saying he wanted Pierson to lie to the FBI agents if they asked him about the incident. Brooklier explained that what Shane meant on the recording was that he wanted Pierson to not tell the truth about the growing of the marijuana. He inferred that information could hurt him in acquiring his MBA and ultimately a good paying job.

Further, he harped on the fact that the Vegas witnesses claimed to have seen Ben and Adar alive in their stores in Las Vegas. None of these witnesses identified Shane as being in Vegas. Several of the witnesses were certain they saw Frandsen. This was where Brooklier tried to plant the seed that it could have been Frandsen who took the victims to Vegas and somehow killed them, possibly when they were returning to

California. This was where the defense was able to show a giant hole in the prosecution's case. He referred to the fact the prosecution rejects these witnesses because they don't fit into their new theory of the case. Yet these were excellent witnesses, with no baggage like Pierson and Tuttle.

The waiter from the Outback Restaurant had gone on with his career to be a sworn police officer. The other assistant manager from Best Buy examined Adar's passport and other identification, then looked the purchaser in the face, and they appeared to be the same person. The defense exploited the contrast between the civilian witnesses for the prosecution with the defense—which witnesses were credible and made consistent statements.

Brooklier continued to take swipes at Karla by saying that all she was giving the jurors were posters and theories. He said, "I'm talking about the admission by the prosecutor when she stands up here and says there are holes—there's a big hole in this case. ...We don't know who killed whom. Maybe Shane killed 'em. In which case I've got one theory for you. He actually committed the murders. ...Now if you don't believe that, I've got another theory for you. They were killed during the course of a kidnapping....Does she really have the guts to ask you to do that in a double murder case?"

The defense vigorously argued that his client hadn't made incriminating statements to Pierson which were secretly recorded by Pierson. He said the prosecutor, during her argument, had read from the transcript. He told the jurors the following: "There's one big glaring error here and I would like if some of you would care to write this down, I think this is very, very important...Ms. Kerlin read this to you from page 13, line 25.

Pierson says, "Dude, come on dude, I mean you think...I mean it's pretty obvious, I mean it, isn't it? I mean I saw you with the shovel and shit and all that,"

Shane says, "I'm sorry, dude."

Pierson says, "What do you mean, dude? Come on."

Shane says, "You are right, you did, you are right, you did."

Brooklier in his argument said, "I want you to listen to it. You know what Shane Huang actually says? You are lying. Listen for it. He doesn't say, **"You are right."** He says, **"You are lying."**

He urged the jurors to play that portion of the tape when they were deliberating in the jury room and they would be convinced that his client had made no admissions, only denials about his liability with regard to the deaths of the two young men. He repeated this challenge for the jurors to listen to the tape and see that Karla was wrong and he was right. He made this a big deal, as though Karla had made up this incriminating evidence. Karla didn't want to appear to be squirming in her chair, but she had never been attacked like that in front of a jury. Since Brooklier was so definite, Karla started to question whether the transcriber had made a mistake and she hadn't caught it.

Brooklier did a masterful job of getting the sentencing information before the jury. He did it in an indirect way by talking about Tuttle. He wanted the jurors to know that if they convicted Shane, he would spend the rest of his life in prison. Brooklier was asking the jurors if they would convict a person of double murder based on Pierson's testimony. "You go to jail for the rest of your life without possibility of parole. Would you really do that to another human being based on this lousy testimony from this liar?"

Brooklier had about 15 minutes more to argue, and it was getting late. So the judge recessed the proceedings until the morning. Karla hurriedly jumped out of her chair and went back to her office. She cued up the tape recorder to again listen to the tape to see if the defense attorney was correct. Upon listening to the tape, it was crystal clear that the defense attorney was wrong, and in fact, Shane had admitted that Pierson was right that he had gotten the rope in shovel from Home Depot. On the tape you could clearly hear Shane say the following: **"You are right, you did, you are right, you did."**

She had not misstated the evidence. In fact, it was clear that the defense attorney was completely wrong. This was a major relief to Karla. Karla wondered how the defense attorney was going to explain his mistake as to the tape. The next morning, Brooklier barely mentioned the tape and his so-called estimate of 15 minutes left to argue turned into over an hour. When Karla stood up to do her 'Rebuttal Argument,' she could see in the jurors' eyes they were saturated with facts from both arguments. She knew she had to be quick with her rebuttal because the jurors' interest span was about to snap.

Karla didn't do a "I gotcha" but pointed out that she definitively wanted the jurors to play the tape because the defendant clearly states that Pierson was correct in that Shane did have the shovel and rope. She didn't try to make Brooklier look bad. Apparently the defense attorney never checked the tape but relied on the defendant's representation that he made no admissions.

Karla condensed her 'Rebuttal Argument' into one chart she put on the easel. It was titled **"Where Evidence Points."** The jurors seemed to focus in on this 'Arrow Chart.' She used it to summarize the points that she wanted to discuss in her 'Rebuttal.' Karla liked to finish her argument by showing how the evidence pointed to this particular defendant. This was an effective way to show on one page how much evidence there was and that it all pointed to defendant, Shane Huang. It had nine arrows all pointing to a photo of Shane in the center of the chart.

As she was progressing with her Rebuttal, she could sense that the jurors were listening. Some of them were taking notes, but everyone was paying attention to her every word. The evidence was overwhelming that Shane had the strongest motive to harm Ben. The attempt by the defense to lay both killings on Frandsen was a hard sell. Frandsen had no motive to kill the victims, plus he had no car to use to get rid of the bodies. There was no way that Frandsen could carry off these murders by himself. When looking at both of their personalities, Frandsen was merely a 'follower' while Shane was clearly the 'leader.'

Brooklier had fired numerous personal attacks at Karla, especially her using over 50 visual displays to help the jurors understand the facts and the law. In one particular attack, he grabbed a chart lying against the courtroom wall and flung it around in the air. He told the jurors how flimsy it was with all the bends and scratches on it. He said that it was an illustration of how weak and flimsy the prosecution's case was. Karla had to admit that some of the poster boards were bent. She explained that her law clerk only had a small car and the trunk lid had slightly crunched the larger charts when he was transporting charts from downtown to the Van Nuys courthouse.

Karla reversed the argument by saying the prosecution tried to help the jurors with their job of understanding a complex case, with multiple defendants and multiple victims. Then she compared her 50 visuals to the three small posters the defense used throughout the trial. By that time, the jurors were smiling and nodding as Karla took her last poster off the easel and sat down at the counsel table indicating that the time for Argument was over.

(On the following graphic page are two of the Argument charts used by the prosecutor.)

Graphic 12

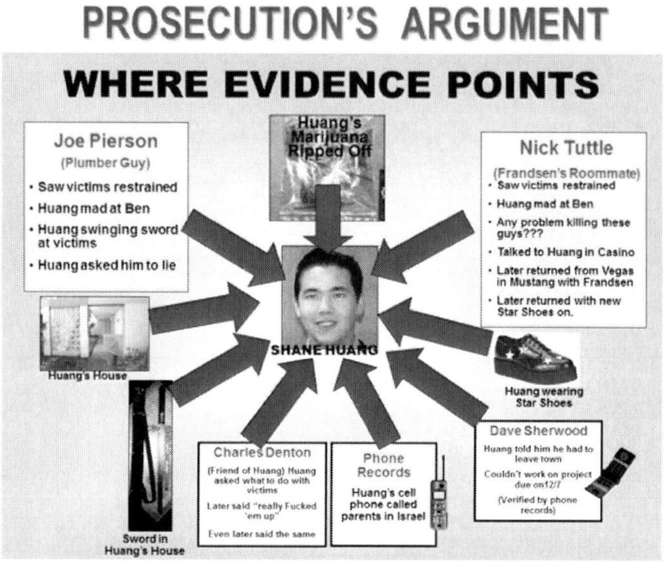
PROSECUTION'S ARGUMENT
WHERE EVIDENCE POINTS
Joe Pierson
(Plumber Guy)
• Saw victims restrained
• Huang mad at Ben
• Huang swinging sword at victims
• Huang asked him to lie
Huang's Marijuana Ripped Off
Nick Tuttle
(Frandsen's Roommate)
• Saw victims restrained
• Huang mad at Ben
• Any problem killing these guys???
• Talked to Huang in Casino
• Later returned from Vegas in Mustang with Frandsen
• Later returned with new Star Shoes on.
SHANE HUANG
Huang's House
Huang wearing Star Shoes
Sword in Huang's House
Charles Denton
(Friend of Huang) Huang asked what to do with victims
Later said "really Fucked 'em up"
Even later said the same
Phone Records
Huang's cell phone called parents in Israel
Dave Sherwood
Huang told him he had to leave town
Couldn't work on project due on12/7
(Verified by phone records)

WHAT HAPPENED ON THE WAY TO LAS VEGAS?
Driver
Huang's Car
SHANE HUANG
Victims Buried at Afton Canyon Campground
LAS VEGAS
Driver
Wertzberger's Car
BENJAMIN FRANDSEN
Ben Wertzberger
Adar Ne'eman
Huang & Frandsen left Wertzberger's car in Las Vegas with key & luggage inside it

CHAPTER 32—VERDICT AND SENTENCING

The jury room buzzer rang out loud and clear in the courtroom, indicating the jury had reached a verdict. Then the mad scramble began as the courtroom clerk quickly grabbed her telephone to notify everyone that the jury had reached a verdict. She advised all the parties to return to court for the reading of the verdict. The defense attorney was immediately notified. He had to be ecstatic that the jury had reached a verdict. Throughout the trial, the defense attorney had been triumphant on many of the legal issues. The court watchers had speculated that Shane's attorney had been paid a million dollars for his representation of Shane.

No one could have been more confident of a 'not guilty' verdict than Shane and his attorney. The notion has always been that a quick verdict was a good sign for the defense. The defendant was thrilled. Shane had to believe that it had been worth every penny he had spent on the defense. Shane had been in custody for a long time, and this could mean he would soon be a free man.

Shane was so confident as to the outcome, he had made reservations for dinner for himself, his family, and his girlfriend for that evening at one of the most elegant and pricey restaurants in Beverly Hills. He wanted to celebrate his victory and enjoy something different from jailhouse cuisine. Shane was in a great mood, and he looked upon himself as a winner. When he sauntered back into the courtroom, he waved and smiled at his family and friends. The defendant's family included his father and his step-mother, both of whom had flown in from Taiwan. Shane's mother, who lived in the San Francisco Bay area, was also present.

When Karla had gotten the word there was a verdict, she proceeded to the courtroom and took her seat at counsel table all by herself. She knew the victims' families were waiting for justice to be served and the TV cameras were there to record the outcome. It seemed that this case had generated a lot of interest in the Van Nuys courthouse. A number of the local judges had also wandered into the courtroom for the reading of the verdict. There were other attorneys and law enforcement officials who packed the courtroom. While seated at the counsel table, Karla gradually turned her head, and all she could see was a wall of faces staring in her direction. She wished she could be some other place in the world besides this courtroom, at this moment in time.

Karla and everyone from the DA's Office knew that this was a very difficult case for the prosecution. Karla knew that she had done the best job she could under the circumstances, especially since she had such a limited time to prepare. The case was extremely dependent on circumstantial evidence. It would be so difficult to get 12 jurors to follow the trail of evidence and not be distracted by sympathy for the defendant and the lack of any direct evidence as to who did the killing. Karla had earlier hoped for a hung jury so that Shelly Samuel, the original prosecutor, could later retry Shane's case jointly with Frandsen's case.

All the courtroom seats were filled, and in the back people were standing, blocking the courtroom door. As the judge entered, the bailiff called the courtroom to order. The judge sat down in her chair and directed the clerk to have the jurors brought into the courtroom to take their respective seats. As the jury filed into the courtroom, Karla carefully looked at them to see if any body language would indicate which way the verdict may have gone. But Karla couldn't get a reading from the jurors. The judge asked the jury if they had reached a verdict. The foreperson indicated that they had and was told to hand the verdict forms to the bailiff. As the bailiff was handing the verdicts to the judge, there was a flicker of a smile on Shane's face. It would be less than a minute before the defendant would hear his fate for the rest of his life. The possibility of Shane walking out the courtroom's double doors and into the arms of his girlfriend was moments away from becoming a reality.

The judge gave the verdict forms to the court clerk to read. The clerk cleared her throat and tried to raise her voice so all could hear as she stated, "We, the jury in the above entitled action find the defendant Shane Huang guilty of **First Degree Murder of Ben Wertzberger."** This was repeated again as to victim Adar Ne'eman.

Who was stunned the most? Karla drew upon her showgirl skills and looked stoically straight ahead without showing any emotion. Shane and his attorney seemed to go into shock, with Shane shaking his head in slow motion mouthing the words, "No, no."

Karla pretended to be writing in the DA's file in front of her. She was surprised and tried to collect her thoughts. There was no doubt in her mind that Shane was guilty, but it had been such an uphill fight to try to get the witnesses to come to court. She had tried so hard to present the facts of the case to the jurors in a cogent manner in order to convince them that the defendant was guilty. She tried to remain poised and not show any jubilation over the fact that the defendant was found guilty of two counts of Murder.

After the verdicts had been read, the defendant looked stunned and dejected. The bailiff came over to his chair and motioned for him to get up. Shane was then escorted to the custody door, and he was heard to say to the bailiff, **"I guess that means I won't be able to make my dinner reservations in Beverly Hills."**

(The following graphic page shows a disappointed Shane Huang over dinner reservations. The remaining photos show the author at the various sites and how they look today.)

THE DEFENDANT HAD DINNER PLANS

To show how confident Huang was he told his girlfriend that after the verdict he had made dinner reservations for them & his mother at the La Scala Restaurant in Beverly Hills

JURY CAME BACK WITH MURDER VERDICT

Shane Huang

I guess that means I won't be able to make my dinner reservations in Beverly Hills.

YEARS LATER

Author at the rear of the De Soto House

Author at Afton Campground

Author at Grave site in rear of Campground

Graphic 13

CHAPTER 33—DELIBERATIONS

After the verdict was announced in court, the judge thanked the jurors for serving and they were excused and permitted to leave. They were told they could talk to the attorneys if they would like but they were not obligated to do so. After Karla had finished up in court, she walked into the court hallway and saw most of the jurors standing around conversing with one another. Karla knew this was her chance to see what had really swayed the jurors. Karla asked the jurors how they reached their verdict. The women jurors' eyes lit up and they were eager to talk to Karla. They were excited that one of the attorneys was interested in learning how they arrived at their verdict.

They explained that when they started their deliberations they were split down the middle. Half of the jurors didn't want Shane to spend the rest of his life in prison. These six jurors felt it would be a waste of the defendant's talents to not have an opportunity to contribute to society. These jurors wouldn't have hesitated to convict a gang member or "a lowlife" of the murder charge. However, when it came to this young, well-educated Asian young man, these jurors seemed to require a higher standard of proof.

Even though there wasn't supposed to be a different level of proof, the defense attorney during the Argument very astutely mentioned the potential sentence his client would receive if convicted was life in prison without the possibility of parole.

The Defense Attorney was able to inform the jury of the possible sentence during questioning of the witness Nick Tuttle. It was mentioned that it would be the sentence Tuttle could receive if he didn't agree to the plea bargain.

Six of the jurors, who believed Shane was guilty, started to go over the evidence to see if the other jurors were willing to change their minds. The jurors didn't place much weight in the testimony of the witnesses from Las Vegas. Some jurors said that they didn't know for certain whether the defendant had gone to Las Vegas, or even been involved in the burying of the victims. The jurors relied on the fact that the defendant had the greatest motive to kill Ben Wertzberger.

Several of the jurors told Karla they appreciated the visuals that she had prepared for them. The visual that was most helpful to the jurors was the **Clock Timeline Charts**. It showed no phone activity between Shane and Frandsen when they were together killing the victims, and the other time when there was no phone activity was when the two of them were digging the grave.

Karla had outsmarted the defense attorney in having these charts marked as exhibits and later received into evidence at the end of the trial. She knew that if the jurors had these charts to use in their deliberations they would be better able to visualize how the phone records supplied the corroboration of Shane's guilt.

As it turned out, Karla had been right on point. The jurors used her exhibits to bring around the other 'not-guilty' jurors. It wasn't long before the jurors were split only 11 to1. There was one lady juror who just didn't want to believe that the defendant had been involved in the murders.

During the Argument, the defense attorney had picked up one of Karla's charts and said that it contained speculation and not facts. The defense attorney went on to claim that there could be 20 other explanations for what actually happened. During her 'Rebuttal Argument,' Karla picked up the chart the defense had attacked. She turned to the jurors and said that the defense counsel claimed there were 20 other explanations. Then she asked the jury, "Did he tell you any of those explanations?" Rhetorically, she answered her question. She said that the reason you didn't hear any other explanations was the fact that there wasn't any other reasonable explanation than that Shane and Frandsen killed the victims and went to Vegas.

Later in the deliberations, the one hold-out juror remembered that at no time did the defense attorney offer even one explanation. That seemed to be a pivotal point for her. The group of women jurors indicated that when the defense attorney attacked Karla's charts as mere cardboard, they wondered, if he had such a good case, then why hadn't he prepared charts for his Argument? They interpreted the lack of visual aids to mean that the defense didn't have anything to counter the evidence presented by the prosecution.

After one and one half days of deliberation, the last holdout juror agreed that there was sufficient evidence to prove the defendant was guilty. She still didn't like the fact that the defendant would be subject to such a harsh sentence.

Karla listened to those jurors. She was thankful that she had used the 50 prosecution exhibits, compared to the three exhibits used by the defense. Karla reflected on her showgirl career and remembered that when she use to be backstage and hear them yell out the word "SHOWTIME," you put on a happy face and gave the audience (Jury) your best performance under the conditions that existed.

CHAPTER 34—EPILOGUE

Frandsen's case was tried by prosecutor Shelly Samuels after she had tried the Blake case. In Frandsen's jury trial, he took the witness stand and tried to downplay his role in the killings. The jury was not convinced by his testimony, and he was convicted of two First Degree Murders. Frandsen appealed his conviction, and a California appellate court reversed it on the grounds that the judge had improperly instructed the jury on the elements of multiple murder, special circumstance, the natural and probable consequences doctrine, and involuntary manslaughter. He was retried, and this time Frandsen was convicted of **Second Degree Murder**.

Shane appealed his conviction and argued he had had ineffective counsel. Shane was very critical of his defense attorney, Brooklier, whom he allegedly paid a million dollars to represent him. Shane claimed his attorney had promised the jurors during his opening statement that they would hear from two defense witnesses who would testify that Frandsen had admitted that he had murdered the victims. However, his attorney failed to produce those witnesses. He also claimed that Brooklier's cross-examination was inadequate, as to Pierson. He further claimed during his closing argument that Brooklier misrepresented the content of the recorded conversation with Pierson. Lastly, Shane stated that his defense attorney failed to adjust the defense to counteract the prosecutor's reliance on a felony-murder theory. After considering all the objections, the appellate court rejected all of Shane's claims as being without merit and upheld his conviction.

As to Karla Kerlin's career, she advanced to be the Special Assistant to the Chief Deputy of the DA's Office. She put in her name for a judgeship and was swiftly appointed as a Superior Court Judge by Governor Schwarzenegger. Presently she sits on the other side of the bench and is handling criminal cases in the downtown Los Angeles courthouse.

Bally's Jubilee performances still are going strong in Las Vegas, although Judge Karla Kerlin is not filling in as one of the "Tall Nudes."

This was an incredible case in which the sun, planets, and moons were in perfect alignment to convict Shane Huang. If any one of the following had not happened, Shane would be walking the streets as a free man:

1. If the victims' mothers hadn't persevered in trying to get someone to take a missing persons report, there wouldn't have been any investigation.

2. If the initial FBI agent hadn't been willing to listen to the mothers, the FBI wouldn't have taken the case.

3. If the agents hadn't started asking questions, Tuttle and Pierson would never have talked.

4. If the agents hadn't gotten the cellphone records, nothing would have been known about who Shane had been talking to.

5. If Agents Clouse and Dempsey hadn't gotten Frandsen to start talking about a possible burial site, no information about the blue-roofed building would have come to light.

6. If the CHP officer hadn't been able to recall the blue-roofed building, the agents wouldn't have known where to look on the road to Vegas.

7. If the cadaver dog hadn't started sniffing at the back of the campsite, the grave wouldn't have been discovered.

8. If Karla Kerlin hadn't been up to the task, the prosecution wouldn't have been able to proceed.

9. If visual exhibits hadn't been used, the jurors most likely wouldn't have understood the facts resulting in a conviction.

10. The list goes on and on, as to all the things that, if they hadn't happened, Shane Huang would be a free man living the Good Life somewhere with his MBA degree from UCLA.

ACKNOWLEDGEMENT

For years I have wanted to write this book because it is the best example of how strong a mother's love can really be for her children. I had a chance to meet the Ne'eman family on one of their many visits they had to make to Los Angeles during the various trials. They are a delightful family whose life revolves around the Israeli dance troupe that they operate. As much as I wanted to contact both families to obtain personal information about their sons, I couldn't bring myself to bother the Ne'eman or Wertzberger families. They have suffered enough, and they don't need me asking personal questions that would only resurface this tragic wound they still have to live with. The information about their sons in this book came from other sources. However, I would be remiss if I didn't acknowledge how much I admire both families and how they handled this heartbreaking situation. They inspire all of us, and I wonder if we could measure up to all they had to do on their own to see that Justice was done in this case.

I believe it is important for society to be aware of the remarkable people who make up our Criminal Justice System. It is always much easier to criticize the police, the attorneys, and even the judges because the media can always find some type of fault with the Justice System. Some people like to second-guess the actions of police officers who have to make spilt-second decisions. A week doesn't go by without some late night TV host making an 'attorney joke' breaking the audience into hilarious laughter. Seldom does anyone say anything positive about the people who actually make the Justice System work on a daily basis.

During my 43-year career as a prosecutor in the Los Angeles County District Attorney's Office, I have had the opportunity to directly work and associate with some incredible people who do their jobs without fanfare and shy away from any attempt to recognize them for a job well done. You the reader have seen from this story the incredible job the FBI did, and they should be commended for it. It is touching to see that such a large federal bureaucratic organization can exhibit such compassion as they did when they assisted these Israeli mothers who were desperately in need of a helping hand.

A special recognition goes to FBI agents David and Kelly, who are amazing individuals, always professional and cooperative. Years ago, I wanted to praise them for a job well done, but they didn't want any attention or recognition. That is why this book doesn't reveal their true names but used pseudonyms instead. They exhibited creativity and ingenuity in solving this double homicide case. Even though murder cases aren't their main forte, they were up to the task and able to outsmart a killer with an MBA who almost got away with murder.

Karla Kerlin was an incredible prosecutor. Since I was the one who hired her as a deputy DA, I feel that I can take part of the credit for her success. I remember her employment application mentioned that she had been a 'Showgirl in Las Vegas.' My reaction was, what a great background, since when you are trying cases in the courtroom it is just like being on stage. I saw Karla grow as an attorney, especially when she handled the worst of the worst rapists and sex offenders. She combines the ability to be well prepared and know how to relate to victims, witnesses, and especially jurors. She is a communicator who knows how to tell a story and make it interesting. Of all the attorneys I have worked with, she was the best listener and recognized what was needed to present a case to the jurors.

My biggest regret with Karla was when she left the DA's Office to become a judge. Super prosecutors are a rare breed, and it takes considerable training and years of experience for them to perfect their necessary skills. District Attorney Steve Cooley was always more philosophical when losing a great prosecutor to becoming a judge. His view was that the DA's Office benefits by having a better group of judges to try their cases in front of. However, I disagree that the loss of an outstanding prosecutor takes years to replace, but I know that Karla will be a great judge.

One last acknowledgement I believe it is necessary to mention is the extraordinary leadership in the DA's Major Crimes Division over the years with head deputies such as Curt Hassel and Pat Dixon. Both resisted any praise for doing an admirable job, but without their insight and tenacity the tough cases wouldn't have been pursued. Curt and later Pat groomed a stable of thoroughbred trial attorneys who were always champing at the bit to take on the most difficult cases in the DA's Office. So many tough cases were successfully prosecuted because of their no-nonsense approach.

What I would like the reader to take from this book is that there are many incredible people who work tirelessly together as a team to makes sure that **JUSTICE** prevails in the American Criminal Justice System.

OTHER BOOKS

By Ronald E Bowers

My original set of books was called the **L. A. True Crime** series. These books highlighted the infamous criminal cases that proceeded through the courtrooms of the Los Angeles Superior Courts.

One of these books was the ***Celebrity Curse.*** This book reviewed the mysterious deaths of celebrities starting with the investigation into **Marilyn Monroe's** death. For over a half a century there has been a growing controversy over her untimely death. Was it an accidental overdose or a suicide? However, over the years more facts have revealed the possibility that she may have been murdered. This book considers all the possibilities trying to separate fact from fiction.

I have included in this book a behind the scenes look at the case of the enablers in the puzzling death of **Anna Nicole Smith** which resulted in one of the most peculiar prosecutions of all times. The ***Celebrity Curse*** further discusses the mysterious deaths of **John Belushi, Natalie Wood** as well as old-time screen legend **Thelma Todd**. Of course, the book wouldn't be complete without including the prosecution of **Michael Jackson's** doctor who was giving the superstar an IV drip of Propofol to assist him in sleeping.

Another aspect of the book ***Celebrity Curse*** is a review of a number to Stalking the Stars cases which include **Madonna, Mel Gibson, Catherine Zeta Jones, John Cusack** and **Steven Spielberg**. Here we discuss the high price of being a celebrity with its loss of privacy and threats to one's life and family members. Without a doubt Stalkers are truly a **CELEBRITY CURSE**.

Another book of the L.A, True Crime series was the ***Death Penalty Designee***. Capital Punishment is considered the third hot button issue after Abortion and Gun Control that most people try to avoid discussing. Everyone has some type of emotional attachment either for or against the Death Penalty without truly understanding the purpose or operation of the Death Penalty. The book doesn't take sides but provides the reader with facts and figures to support their positions. The issues are viewed through the eyes of a person, The Death Penalty Designee, who had to make the ultimate decisions of some of the most notorious cases of all times. The book starts with the Tookie Williams case and continues on with the Richard Ramirez (Night Stalker) case followed by the Bitter and Norris case eventually discussing dozens of homicides that everyone has faded memories of.

Another book was the ***Killings on Route 66***. Part of American history can be told by all who have come west on the old Route 66. This book starts at the very end of Route 66 which is the Santa Monic pier where a number of nefarious cases occurred. Next we travel a few blocks to one of the sites where 10 innocent peoples were slaughtered. We follow Route 66 as it traverses through West Hollywood where Dominick Dunn became inspired to be a celebrated True Crime writer. Further on we come across the most horrific and diabolical double murder of all times in Hollywood. Of course, we touch upon Dr. Haing Ngor's Killing Fields this time of LA as we stop for a deadly Dodger's game. It's amazing that not all the carnage on Route 66 came from traffic accidents.

A long the lines of the previous book was the ***Killers on Mulholland Drive.*** Here I travel down the highway to the Homes of the Stars. I start out relating the sad case of Ennis Cosby who was the victim of a Robbery Gone Bad. Then we weave our way on top of this famous highway to the estate of Marlon Brando where murder raised its ugly head by his son shooting his half-sister's finance while he sat on the sofa watching TV. We can't ignore what happened in his neighbor's house that being Jack Nicholson. That was where Roman Polanski seduced a 14 year old girl and ultimately he became America's most famous fugitive. We examine how this road is Hollywood's Lovers Lane and at times it leads to deadly consequences.

Within this series the most fascinating book was the ***Old Lady Killers***. For so many years I have been inundated with homicide cases involving male suspects. There have been a few female murder cases, but they involved women who generally want to knock off their husbands for the life insurance benefits. It is so rare to see a grandmother type committing crime. However, when I had to work on the Sante Kimes case, I couldn't believe how elderly women could be so evil. Next I worked on the case against Helen Golay (76) and Olga Rutterschmidt (74) who made a living caring for the homeless just to run over them to collect the life insurance policies they took out on these men. This book will definitely change your opinion about sweet little old ladies who can be incredibly malicious and wicked.

Another book of this series was the ***Rich Kid Killers of Beverly Hills.*** This book examines the infamous Billionaire Boys Club killing which was the genesis for the Menendez Brothers massacre of their parents. How could rich kids who have experienced the good life and were well educated turn to murder? Most people think that only the poor or less affluent commit crime. Although rich kids' motives to kill are quite different from the poor or gang shootings, however they do occur and can be difficult to solve.

However, the story in the next book ***Killing in the Castle*** was televised during the first trial. Most readers are familiar with Phil Spector, the music producer, who brought us the 'Wall of Sound' and who was accused of killing an actress in his castle/house. However, few people know the true story of how this case labeled the 'Battle of the Experts' resulted in a hung jury. This case illustrates what happens when the defendant has unlimited resource and can hire dozens of Defense attorneys to represent him.

For the auto racing fans, the next book ***Killing of a Legend*** will be most noteworthy. The double murder case of Mike Thompson the famous auto racing legend and his wife was one of the longest Unsolved Mysteries. A fledgling energetic Sheriff's detective took a new look at this old case and followed up on some obscure facts that unlocked the key to this case. This is a book about two men with giant egos in which one couldn't accept defeat. They took their disagreement all the way to the U.S. Supreme Court.

Finally, the book that started this L. A. True Crime series was the ***Killer at the Door***. It discusses one of those cases in which the DA's Office prosecuted the wrong suspect. This doesn't happen often but when it does the DA's Office wants to write the wrong and get the real culprit. The facts involved a typical child custody dispute over visitation rights. How can such a matter escalate to the point of hiring a killer to shoot the other ex-spouse? This case has so many twists and turns that you the reader will never feel the same when you open your front door late at night.

My other book series is the **DA Delta Force** series which provides the reader an inside look at several of the extraordinary prosecutors who were assigned to the Major Crimes Division of the Los Angeles County District Attorney's Office. These prosecutors were given the toughest cases and with their meticulous preparation and remarkable litigation skills they were able to bring justice for the victims.

The first DA Delta Force book in the series was titled the ***Prosecutrix Fight for Justice***, in which I discussed Eleanor Hunter, who demonstrated a No Fear attitude in taking on the toughest cases. She demonstrated an uncanny resolve to see that the old Symbionese Liberation Army terrorists were brought to justice for a bank robbery-murder that had been overlooked for years. It took a lot of courage on her part to stand up for what was right.

Other books in this series are ***The Top Gun DA*** starring John Monahan, who was a phenomenal prosecutor. He had the talent to work with detectives and to construct solid cases that could stand up in court. Elite units like the Delta Force have learned that it takes a team effort to win the battle. Prosecutor Monahan had the foresight to know what evidence was needed and how to use that evidence to be persuasive to the jury. He never wavered, even when some of the deadliest killers would give him the 'evil eye.'

Another in this series is the ***Best of the Best DA*** which discusses two remarkable prosecutors, Tony Manzella as well as Hoon Chun, who never gave up when everything seemed to be going wrong with their cases. Prosecutor Manzella stood up to the Mexican Mafia and recognized that the Achilles' heel of this band of gangsters was their self-imposed Green Light. Tony was 'one of a kind.' When he walked into the courtroom, he exuded the confidence of a Philadelphia Lawyer (the lawyer who knows the most detailed and minute points of law) while at the same time he possessed 'Street Smarts.'

As to Prosecutor Hoon Chun, he demonstrated unlimited resolve as he had to deal with crisis after crisis in the Timothy McGhee (Big Bad Dude) case. Hoon had the mindset to see that the 'glass was always half full' when it was practically empty. I told him to his face that there was no way he would be able to convict a paraplegic for committing robbery/murder. Well, he quickly proved me wrong in the Cruz case and got the killer sentenced to state prison.

This DA Delta Force series concludes with ***The Superstar Prosecutor***, which highlighted three astonishing prosecutors, Darrell Mavis and Jeff Ramseyer as well as Michael Camacho. Each was highly talented, but at the same time they were acutely sensitive to the needs of their witnesses. Prosecutor Mavis was a legal genius who was like a chess player thinking three moves ahead. Putting aside his intellect, he had a practical side of knowing how to get things done.

Prosecutor Ramseyer was a remarkable prosecutor who would have left a long legal legacy if it hadn't been for his untimely death. The DA's Office was lucky to have him the short time that he was a part of the DA's Office.

However, Prosecutor Camacho could best be described as an unassuming workaholic. He tried and convicted more gangbangers than any other prosecutor. He truly has made many communities safer places to live by reducing the gang violence. Camacho is the type of prosecutor I wish we could clone since he embodies all the marvelous qualities an attorney should have.

Made in United States
North Haven, CT
04 November 2026

21769092R00113